10 SIMPLE PRINCIPLES OF A HEALTHY DIET

How to Lose Weight, Look Young
and Live Longer

SERGEY YOUNG

10 SIMPLE PRINCIPLES OF A HEALTHY DIET: How to Lose Weight, Look Young and Live Longer / by Sergey Young.

In addition to the paperback edition, this book is available as an eBook and in the Adobe PDF format.

CONTENT

66

**Changing what you eat
is the first step towards
living a longer, better,
and healthier life**

CHAPTER 1

INTRODUCTION

Food is a funny thing. We all eat it—all need it—yet many of us have complicated, if not fraught, relationships with it. This book is here to fix that. And hopefully to help you live to be at least 100 years old—a healthy 100 at that. Changing what you eat is the first step towards living a longer, better, and healthier life. It can improve everything from your appearance and health to your relationships and finances. This might sound too simple and too good to be true, but it's real.

In decades to come, technological breakthroughs will play a leading role in extending our life spans. But that's only worthy of celebration if you can live long enough to see them come to fruition. With regard to living longer, seemingly small choices like what you have for lunch or dinner add up in dramatic fashion over the course of decades. You may not see the effects of poor eating immediately, but eventually you will. That's the bad news. The good news is that the same can be said for good eating habits. They'll add up and, in turn, help stave off disease and extend your life. You'll have more energy and less illness. You'll be more productive and motivated. And you'll have more years on Earth to do the things you love with the people you love.

You're probably thinking: That sounds great, but why should I believe this guy? He's not a doctor or a scientist. But here's the thing: many years of practice is another way to become an expert. I've spent years studying healthy eating in order to hack my health and extend my life. I would argue that the proliferation of so-called experts has played a large role in confusing people about the "right" way to eat. A new diet fad based on a new scientific discovery seems to make the rounds every few months. One day, fat is the devil and the next day, it's the foundation of health. No wonder people are lost!

Now while I haven't uncovered an easy trick to help you live to be 1,000 or patented a super-food recipe to cure the world's major illnesses, I have simply realized—through firsthand experience and research—that changing our daily habits is a huge part of the equation for helping us live longer. It's not rocket science; it starts with food.

WHO IS SERGEY YOUNG?

For me, though, it actually started with something else: a doctor's visit. I had an experience that far too many people have had: blood test results (in my case, high cholesterol) that led to a doctor telling me I had to take a pill every day for the rest of my life. Before this, I was working long hours in consulting, exercised rarely, and didn't think much about what I put in my body or how it affected me. I wasn't alone. For many of us, health feels elusive. Around 70 percent of Americans take at least one prescription drug a day, and the majority take two. Meanwhile, nearly 40 percent of Americans are obese. Not only does obesity lie at the root of everything from type 2 diabetes to heart disease, but it costs individuals an extra $1,429 in medical costs each year.

The prospect of taking a pill every day until my death felt unnatural to me, so I began doing some research. That was when I started to see just how common it was for people to be struggling with their physical health—and when I began to realize there was a surprisingly easy first step towards a more appealing way of life. Fast forward a few years and what started as a journey to figure out how I could lower my cholesterol without taking medicine has morphed into a broader question—

one that now drives and consumes my whole career. How can we all live longer, healthier lives?

I like to think my experience and dedication to this topic lends me a little extra credibility. And if telling you more about myself will help you take my advice more seriously, I'm happy to do it. I've been an investor for over 20 years. I launched a fund to invest in longevity-focused companies and am leading an XPRIZE initiative on the topic. I've spent years talking to everyone I could—from some of the smartest people in Boston, who work on AI drug discovery and revolutionary treatments for age-related diseases, to complete strangers—about how we can all live longer. In fact, over the years, I've realized that we already know how to live 100 healthy, happy years. We're just not using this knowledge.

**We already know
how to live 100 healthy,
happy years. We're just not
using this knowledge**

WHY THIS BOOK?

The problem is not that we don't have all the information we need—in fact, there's never been more advice available. But that's a double-edged sword. People are experiencing information overload—too much advice, much of it conflicting. And when people are overwhelmed, they tune out. Is red meat good or bad? Are blueberries actually a superfruit? Should you put butter in your coffee? Are carbs the devil, as the Atkins and keto diets suggest? Or is gluten to blame?

Sometimes, you hear one crazy thing on Monday, and by Friday it's out of fashion. If you try to follow the headlines, you'll likely lose your sanity—and your health definitely won't improve. This book is the antidote. It will make you realize two things. First, eating right is much more important than it seems. Second, it's also much less complicated.

Beyond my investments in healthy longevity, my role in helping everyone live longer is pretty straightforward: simplify, sort through and distill all the important information we already have about health. I'm going to make all the diet advice you've read, ignored, heard, questioned, and forgotten digestible. Let's make it stick. Food is the foundation of everything. And everyone has to eat. So why not extend your life span in the process? Far too often, we outsource our longevity choices, letting doctors, supermarkets, food producers, and advertisers define our health. Sometimes, it might feel like we lack the power to control how we feel. With this book as a guide, you will be able to take back your life.

It offers principles and suggestions, rather than daily plans or complex rules, so you can adapt that digestible information to your own lifestyle and goals.

There are numerous benefits to following the longevity principles—some of which may surprise you. Eating well can improve your digestion, help to reverse everything from autoimmune diseases to high cholesterol and blood pressure, and potentially reduce your reliance on prescription drugs. Eating well will help you look and feel better. You will lose weight; your skin will glow. You will sleep better and thus be more active and energetic through the day.

I personally lost weight. I no longer need the drugs my doctor wanted me to take for the rest of my life, I have way more energy, not only for work but also for spending time with my four hyper active kids, family and friends.

Following longevity diet principles is also good for your financials: you'll save money on drugs, blood tests, and doctor's visits. And as you'll see in the pages to come, the foods I recommend can help you save on your groceries.

Now, I'm not going to overwhelm you with a list of citations that could stretch to the moon. That would be counterintuitive, considering what I said already: the biggest hurdle to healthy eating is information overload. This book is not an encyclopedia. It's short for a reason—so that you can put the intel I've rounded up into practice. And it's not a complex plan to memorize, but principles to make your own.

"

First, eating right is much more important than it seems. Second, it's also much less complicated

**Living longer starts
with eating well, and
eating well starts with
simplicity**

WHAT TO EXPECT

Of course, I could tell you exactly what to eat and you could still choose to ignore this advice. But sometimes, habits don't stick because we subconsciously doubt them. That's why, before I tell you what to eat, I'm going to explain further why it matters.

14 IN CHAPTER 2,

I'll give you the **rundown on longevity** and how it relates to the foods you put on your plate. Then, we'll get to the action.

20 IN CHAPTER 3,

I'll outline **10 longevity diet principles**, with short explanations for each. Next, we'll get a little bit more detailed.

42 IN CHAPTER 4,

I'll dive into **specific foods** and their **health benefits.**

58 IN CHAPTER 5,

I'll tell you **five foods to avoid.**

66 IN CHAPTER 6,

we'll take your health to the next level **with supplements.**

79 FINALLY, IN CHAPTER 7,

I'll show you how this information is all **put into practice** with some examples from my own lifestyle.

In addition to my personal stories, you will notice a few references to a specific group —celebrities and top actors. There is a reason for that. These people have a vested interest in looking and staying young since their careers and ability to make money are directly related to their appearance. They spend more time, money and energy on fighting aging than anyone else on the planet, and I believe their choices and best practices to be worth mentioning in the book.

Pretty simple, right? That's the point. Living longer starts with eating well, and eating well starts with simplicity.

CHAPTER 2

WHAT IS LONGEVITY?

Before we get into what you should (or shouldn't) have for dinner, let's take a minute to talk about this concept of longevity. Longevity is basically your life expectancy or life span—how long you will live. But this book is concerned not only with gaining years, but also improving the quality of those years by strengthening the quality of your health. This concept is sometimes referred to as your health span — the length of time you're healthy, not just alive. We don't currently have a lot of data on the average health span. But thinking of life span and health span is a good way to remember that quantity is important but only alongside quality.

Naturally, there's a lot of talk about the possibility of living forever. My fellow technology investors like Peter Diamandis, MD and Jim Mellon, and scientists like David Sinclair, PhD and Aubrey de Gray, PhD to name just a few, work hard on studying, investing and making longevity discoveries and tools available for the public. And there's a seemingly endless supply of headlines touting the tech innovations that will make immortality a reality. I absolutely believe technology will help us live longer and healthier lives. That's why I invest in it! But I also know some people are made skeptical by the hype. I talk to plenty of people who are excited about the possibility of living longer, but I also meet many who are terrified.

This book is concerned not only with gaining years, but also improving the quality of those years by strengthening the quality of your health

This fear, too, comes from a lack of understanding. That's why I usually like to break longevity into three horizons. While fundamental breakthroughs in technology will be required to help us live to 150 or 200 (or beyond), lifestyle changes are all it takes to tack an extra 10 or 20 years onto your current life expectancy, and to improve the quality of those years in the process. Seems attractive, right?

With a little Health 101, you can live to be 101—and still feel young. This is what I call the first horizon of longevity. Moving your body, avoiding smoking, meditating, and eating well are seemingly obvious health "hacks" that far too many people fail to implement consistently. Don't take my word for it. A Harvard study recently found that abstaining from smoking, with a moderate BMI (body mass index), a quality diet, at least 30 minutes of exercise each day, and low alcohol intake can add 12 years to your life span. In this book, we're going to focus on the "quality diet" part of that equation. Consider it your first class on the first horizon of longevity.

The second horizon of longevity includes innovations like early diagnostics technology and precision medicine (to name just two) that will dramatically improve our ability to fight diseases. While tremendous progress has already been made in this realm, many solutions still need to be verified before they're ready for the mass market. They'll be ready in the next 5, 10 or 15 years. Improving your health the old-fashioned way—by being conscious about what you eat—is a perfect priority in the meantime.

The third horizon of longevity involves an even more dramatic innovation: tech integrated into the human body, such as replaceable or artificial body parts, and internal organs and brain-computer interfaces that will give us the ability to control computers using our thoughts. These possibilities often get the most buzz, but are far off to say the least. To be blunt, you're better off focusing on improving your lifestyle habits than daydreaming about futuristic health solutions. That's why we're here.

FOOD AND LONGEVITY

I am extremely optimistic about our ability to improve health by simply changing how and what we eat. Make the wrong food choices, and you'll increase your risk for a long list of problems, some deadly: cancer, high blood pressure, liver disease, and so on. Make the right ones, and the inverse takes place. However, many of us aren't making the right ones. This year, three-quarters of deaths are expected to be caused by chronic disease. Life expectancy in the U.S. has actually been on the decline in recent years, currently hovering around 80. And as I already mentioned, the vast majority of Americans rely on prescription drugs. Some numbers look awful. Only one in three American children engage in daily physical activity. By 2030, half of Americans are expected to be obese.

In his recent book *Food Fix*, Mark Hyman, MD shares depressing data: "Obesity rates in children have tripled since the 1970s and one in three is overweight or obese. In fact, one in four teenagers now have type 2 diabetes or pre-diabetes—something I never saw in my medical school training 30 years ago. If a child is overweight his life expectancy may be 10-20 years less."

A recent Moody's Analytics report also showed that millennials, now the largest percentage of the population, are "undoubtedly less healthy than the previous generation," as regards both physical and behavioral health (which are closely linked). "Without intervention, millennials could feasibly see mortality rates climb up by more than 40 percent compared to Gen-Xers at the same age," the report states. Translation: we have plenty of room for improvement—and that improvement is an urgent undertaking. But as I've been saying, we also have the recipe for it. It's just a matter of paying attention to what's already working for people, then putting that into practice on an everyday basis.

We need to extend healthy lifestyles from isolated areas to the whole planet, and that entails creating healthy communities within our families and workplaces

Researchers have conducted many twin studies to separate nature from nurture and have concluded that genetics is only the root of 20 to 30 percent of health. The rest is lifestyle—and your lifestyle can be changed. It's obvious whose lifestyle you should imitate. The world is full of these types of idols. A centenarian, for one, is someone who lives past 100. And between 1980 and 2010, the number of centenarians rose by 66 percent. One centenarian named Mary Todisco told the *New York Daily News* her secret. It honed in on the lifestyle choice we're talking about here: diet. "I watch my weight—no sugar, honey," she said. Indeed, one-quarter of centenarians surveyed said adhering to a healthy diet helped them live to be 100.

Japan has one of the highest centenarian ratios in the world. There, 48 out of every 100,000 people live to 100, compared to 22 out of every 100,000 in the U.S. Of course, it's easier if you're surrounded by people engaging in the same healthy lifestyle. Often, concentrations of centenarians are in places where nature creates an environment that's auto-set to healthy choices. Sometimes, they're literally islands. We need to extend healthy lifestyles from isolated areas to the whole planet, and that entails creating healthy communities within our families and workplaces. Google is a great example of a company that's ensuring the environment is geared for good health; its campuses contain everything from fitness centers and bikes to doctors and healthy food options. You already eat every day. You might as well do it right. So, what does "right" look like? Let's dig in.

CHAPTER 3

LONGEVITY DIET

PRINCIPLES

Take the test here: sergeyyoung.com/ diet-test

The first step is to check on your current diet habits. Here's a simple and comprehensive test I created to help you get perspective on how longevity-focused your diet is now.

Before you head to the store to restock your fridge, we need to lay the foundation for your longevity diet. All the people I've talked to, and all the things I've read and researched, overlap tremendously. I've boiled the basics down into 10 principles. Absorbing and understanding these principles is more important than trying to follow an elaborate diet. Most diets tend to fail long term. Instead, you should interpolate these principles in a way that works for you. Incorporate them into your lifestyle and use them as your compass—your guiding light. In doubt about a food decision? Think about these principles and how your choice fits in. You will know what to do. Here is a simple infographic you can print out and stick on your fridge as an everyday reminder.

Download infographic here: sergeyyoung.com/10-longevity-diet-principles

10 LONGEVITY DIET PRINCIPLES

Sergey Young

1 THE MORE PLANTS, THE BETTER

EAT:
- as many plant-based meals as possible
- rainbow of colors: green, red, orange, yellow and white veggies, fruits and berries
- whole plants, not processed

2 CHECK YOUR FOOD SOURCES

CHOOSE:

- organically grown produce
- hormone-free meat and poultry
- wild fish and seafood
- local, seasonal and farm-grown food

3 STAY AWAY FROM PROCESSED FOODS

Processed foods are created for adictive consumption, and are full of harmful artificial ingredients and added sugar

4 AVOID SWEETS AND PASTRY

SAY NO TO:
- all obvious sweets and deserts
- hidden sugar in sauces and condiments, processed and fast foods
- wheat products: bread, cookies, pastas, etc.

5 ADD OLIVE OIL

Use cold-pressed olive oil instead of strore-bought dressings, sauces and condiments. Olive oil contains healthy fats and anti-oxidants

6 EAT EARLY IN THE DAY

Frontload your day, i.e. make breakfast the heaviest meal

7 CONSIDER INTERMITTENT FASTING

Fasting activates our survival circuit that serves to keep us alive and healthy for longer

EXAMPLES:
- don't eat 1 day a week
- don't eat for 18 or 16 hours each day

8 FALL IN LOVE WITH WATER

- replace soda, sugary drinks and coffee with water
- start your day with a glass of water
- keep some water on your desk and take sips each hour

9 CONSUME COFFEE AND WINE IN MODERATION

It's ok to have
- 1 or 2 espresso shots a day
- 1 or 2 glasses of wine per weekend

10 DECIDE ON DAIRY

If you go for dairy, choose organic. But we recommend you::
- replace dairy with plant milk
- try soy products

Connect with me on:

Website: sergeyyoung.com

 Facebook: sergeyyoung200

 Linkedin: Sergey Young

DOWNLOAD THIS INFOGRAPHIC HERE: WWW.SERGEYYOUNG.COM/INFOGRAPHICS

THE MORE PLANTS, THE BETTER

Eating plants is the best thing you can do for your health, hands down. Plants are the best medicine, contain fewer calories, and are less expensive to eat. Food writer Michael Pollan simplified healthy eating, arguably better than anyone else, which is why he continues to be quoted by other food writers (me included!) time and time again. "Eat food, not too much, mostly plants." Any diet that helps you live longer absolutely must emphasize plants. This is the base of your food pyramid—the foundation of each and every meal. To start with, plants have far fewer calories per bite than animal products like meat, fish, and eggs—and caloric restriction has been shown to be linked to your life span.

In *A Short Guide to a Long Life*, David Agus, MD suggests at least five servings of fruits and vegetables a day. His logic: the more plants you consume, the less room on your plate for junk options. Michelle Obama agrees: "I tell my kids, as long as you eat fruits and vegetables at every meal, you'll be okay if you have pizza or ice cream every once in a while. The problem is when the treats become the habits."

Also, plants tend to serve as a crucial medicine. We'll get into the specifics more in the next chapter, but plants are powerful to say the least. They can help you avoid chronic diseases and obesity. Some can help reverse insulin resistance and heart disease. Green leafy vegetables help detox your liver. Blueberries contain anti-aging properties. And if you are not against saving some money, you will be happy to know that plant-based diets are estimated to cost $750 less per year, according to a study in the *Journal of Hunger & Environmental Nutrition*.

Another piece of advice that comes from many nutritionists and is supported by, among others, 66-year-old supermodel Christie Brinkley, suggests we eat vegetables of different colors or a "rainbow of colors". Brinkley shares: "For many, many, many years, I've always said: 'go for as many colors as possible in a day.' That's my main concept for making sure my kids get all the nutrients—making sure the deep greens, yellows and reds and purples, all of that."

All you need to remember is this: the plan is to eat more plants. Add them to each meal. My typical breakfast is homemade granola with a handful of berries and seeds or eggs with avocado. I always have either broccoli, cauliflower, asparagus, zucchini or other vegetables as a garnish for lunch and dinner. My favorite salad is made of cucumbers, tomatoes and lettuce. If I snack I opt for berries, nuts or fresh veggies. I also try to teach everyone around me about the benefits of plants and use every opportunity to feed my kids with plant based meals.

**Keep it simple:
the fewer ingredients
on the label, the better**

STAY AWAY FROM PROCESSED FOODS

There is a very important nuance: when I talk about plants I mean whole plants. And that brings us to the second principle for a longevity diet. Stay away from processed foods even if they are plant based, like French fries, chips, pizzas or fruit juices. This links back to caloric restriction. Processed foods add around 500 calories per day to your diet. These foods are often dense in calories since things like sugar are added, and they're engineered to keep you coming back for more. Pringles even put it in their slogan: "Once you pop, you don't stop"! These foods also come packed with toxins and other harmful ingredients. Deli meats, for one, are loaded full of gluten, nitrites (which can cause cancer), and hydrogenated fats. As Dr. Josh Axe wrote in *Eat Dirt*, even supposedly healthy packaged (read: processed) foods are full of additives.

Supermodel Cindy Crawford's number one diet rule is simple: cut out processed foods and replace them with whole foods. I bet this is her secret to looking 20 years younger (in 2020, she celebrated her 54th birthday).

Keep it simple: the fewer ingredients on the label, the better. To that end, you know something's far from processed if it's raw. When I shop for groceries, I try to stay away from foods that have more than one ingredient. Think of these simple examples: extra virgin olive oil (and other cold pressed oils) vs Cesar salad dressing; fish steak vs fish patties.

In a nutshell, add more raw foods and avoid processed ones.

KNOW WHERE YOUR FOOD COMES FROM

Another component of any longevity diet is being aware of the source of your food. Most conventional meats are pumped with steroids, hormones, and antibiotics. When you consume meat and poultry, make sure it's grass-fed certified, organic, and (if possible) local.

Similarly, with fish—which you should opt for over meat as much as possible—make sure it's wild-caught. One health study has followed 96,000 Americans for the last 17 years. It found that people who ate a plant-based diet with a small daily portion of fish lived the longest. But while eating fish can help prevent everything from heart disease to stroke, farmed fish is more likely to include toxins. Many aquaculture operations, as fish farms are called, rely heavily on hormones and antibiotics, just like animal and poultry farms. The takeaway? Know the source, and opt for eating meat and fish only if it's organic and the animal lived a relatively natural, happy life. I love fish and sea food and usually choose wild salmon, herring, sardines and seabrass among others—these fish are very rich in omega-3 fatty acids, less contaminated with mercury, and simply delicious.

Knowing the source, and staying as close to it as possible, is important for your veggies too. Microbes in the local soil can help you better digest foods, improving gut health, which is linked to your immune system and inflammation. Another way to think of these last two principles is to opt for "slow food"—food in which the origin is known and sustainable and (unless it's raw) takes time to prepare—over "fast food."

It is difficult to argue with my dear colleague, board-certified neurologist and bestselling author David Perlmutter, who says that "one of the most challenging aspects of making healthy lifestyle change is finding trustworthy products. Many products in supermarkets today lack transparency in how they are created, contain harmful additives, antibiotics, or pesticides, or are nutrient-poor due to low quality agricultural practices."

Make sure you read the labels on the products you purchase and spend some time researching the best grocery stores and food delivery services in your area.

LONGEVITY DIET PRINCIPLE 4

REMOVE: CANDY, SWEETS, AND BREAD

Fast food doesn't just mean McDonald's or a microwave meal. It also includes other grab-and-go processed foods like bread, which are low in essential nutrients and often contain antinutrients. In fact, bread is considered an ultra-processed food, along with chocolate bars and breakfast cereals. And ultra-processed foods have been shown to increase the risk of early death from all causes. It might be tempting and convenient to grab two slices of white bread and slap some deli meat on it, but those are the kind of short-term choices that will weigh on your life span. In addition to removing bread from your diet—which far too many people consume almost every meal—candy and sweets simply must go. Everything in moderation? Not so fast. Foods that are extremely high in carbohydrates will keep you coming back for more, and that, in turn, will harm your health.

Make sure you read the labels on the products you purchase and spend some time researching the best grocery stores and food delivery

Fast food is often accompanied by sugary drinks, which are just as bad. The more you drink, the greater the risk. Research has shown that there's a 7 percent increased risk of death from any cause for each additional 12 ounces of sugary drink you consume.

Meanwhile, sugar has been linked to diabetes, of course, and obesity, which itself is linked to 13 types of cancer. That's why this principle of longevity keeps things simple: remove these foods from your diet, and don't look back. You get plenty of carbs from whole grains, fruits and vegetables anyway!

Almost a decade ago, a diagnosis of pre-diabetes made actor Alec Baldwin reassess his eating habits. "I stopped eating refined sugars, desserts and sweets," he says. "I've eaten sugar in some fruit. I just try and eat berries. Candy, gum, mints, ice cream, cake, pie, that's all gone. I lost 35 pounds," he told *USA Today*.

Since I adapted longevity diet principles, I skip not only desserts and obvious sweets but also avoid all sugary drinks, fruit juices (even freshly squeezed), all salad dressings, marinades and ketchup that are not homemade, energy bars and "healthy" snacks. I suggest you try it and see how you feel.

LONGEVITY DIET PRINCIPLE 5

ADD IN: OLIVE OIL

Many people clean up their diet yet don't realize they're still consuming common longevity killers—like sugar and unhealthy fats—because of the sauces they put on top of a seemingly healthy lunch or dinner. The shortcut? Add cold pressed olive oil to your diet—and use it to replace those sneaky sauces. Olive oil is anti-inflammatory and can help fight everything from Alzheimer's to cancer.

Olive oil is also central to the Mediterranean diet, which is often highlighted as the ideal mix of foods. Plus, by turning to olive oil as your go-to topping, you'll avoid the sugar and high-fructose corn syrup hiding in ketchup, for instance, or refined vegetable oils found in most mayonnaise options.

This principle also goes back to the idea of avoiding processed foods. Next time you're at the grocery store, glance at the ingredients list of your current favorite salad dressing or condiment... then compare it to what's in olive oil. Hint: it's just olive oil—no sulfites or benzoates (chemical food preservatives) to be found.

When you eat—
not how much or what—
can also play a large role

EAT EARLY IN THE DAY

As already mentioned, caloric restriction has been shown to extend life spans. But *when* you eat—not how much or what—can also play a large role. In fact, this next longevity diet principle puts some emphasis behind the saying that breakfast is the most important meal of the day. Even if you keep the number of calories consistent, front-loading your meals is great for keeping off extra weight, which, once again, is linked to numerous health complications. This is because your digestive system, hormones, and enzymes are most effective during the morning and early afternoon. Your organs slow down at night because your body is preparing for bed. One study, conducted in Spain, had two groups of people eating the same number of calories over the course of five months. Those who ate before 3 p.m. lost far more weight.

This seemingly simple principle is an interesting one because dinner often steals the show culturally. You grab a muffin on the way to work but consume a three-course meal after a long workday. Breaking this habit can make a huge difference. Simply eating more of your calories earlier in the day can help you avoid obesity and its many risk factors.

Since I started eating lunch-like breakfasts on a regular basis, it was easier for me to eat lighter dinners or skip them altogether! In our family, we try to have the last meal before 6 p.m.

CONSIDER INTERMITTENT FASTING

The only thing better than eating a lighter dinner, though, may be skipping dinner altogether. I personally fast for 36 hours every week, from Monday evening until Wednesday morning. But you don't need to go as radical as I do. This book is about adopting these principles in a way that works for you! Having a food window of six, eight, or ten hours a day may be an easier way to start. You consume all your food during that window and fast the rest of the time.

You've probably heard about intermittent fasting by now. There are many variations, though. One of my role models, Harvard professor David Sinclair, recommends skipping one meal a day; meanwhile Yoshinori Nagumo, MD suggests only having one meal per day. Maybe you shrugged off fasting as yet another fad. But early studies are extremely promising.

Fasting can activate our survival circuit, as David Sinclair explains in his book *Lifespan*. The survival circuit is a system that has been in human cells for a long time. And it serves to keep us alive, and healthier for longer, when we're under threat. If you skip a meal, that will raise NAD (Nicotinamide adenine dinucleotide) levels which will activate your sirtuins—protective enzymes, that are the main players in the survival circuit.

One study, conducted on mice, directly linked mice that ate only one meal per day—and thus were intermittent fasting the rest of the time—to having longer life spans.

Whatever way of fasting you decide to adapt, just give it a try. Halle Berry, Kourtney Kardashian, Jennifer Aniston and Gisele Bündchen are already enjoying the many benefits intermittent fasting has to offer.

**The only thing better
than eating a lighter dinner
may be skipping dinner
altogether**

LONGEVITY DIET PRINCIPLE 8

FALL IN LOVE WITH WATER

So far, we've talked mostly about what to eat. But what you drink matters too. It's another area where the list of choices continues to grow, often resulting in confusion. The good news is that this principle is perhaps the simplest of all: drink water. One liter a day? Two liters a day? You decide. The benefits of water are obvious, but one of the biggest ones is that if you fall in love with water, you'll avoid drinks with more sugar and calories. Drinking sugary beverages, according to research, increases the risk of premature death. More specifically, for every 12 ounces of sugary drinks you down each day, there's a 7 percent higher chance of death from any cause and 10 percent higher for cardiovascular disease. This is another instance where moderation is a delusion. But by having water be the foundation of your beverage consumption, you eliminate the number of choices you make and avoid all that harmful sugar.

Staying hydrated through the day is one of the most common tips you hear from leaders of the beauty and wellbeing industry. "I drink a lot of water," is a frequent refrain among celebrities, from Martha Stewart to Kanye West.

I was not used to drinking pure water, so adapting this principle was easier said than done. At some point, I realized that drinking water that is warmer than room temperature is way easier for me than cold or iced water. I can have a sip or two if the water is cold, but a full glass (or even two) when the temperature is around 104°F (40°C). If you have the same challenge drinking water, play with temperature and find your perfect degree.

I start my day with a couple of glasses of warm water and keep a big bottle on my office desk to make sure I stay hydrated.

LONGEVITY DIET PRINCIPLE 9

DECIDE ON DAIRY

This longevity principle is perhaps the greatest gray area of this section. Many people I have spoken to about health do not eat cheese and milk for various reasons. I don't either. It wasn't the biggest change I made in my life, but it's one I would make again. I would tell everyone give it a try. There is a chance you may be intolerant and never realized it. Listen to your body and experiment with opting out of dairy products. Try an elimination diet and see how you feel with dairy out of the equation. Define your relationship with it accordingly.

When I quit dairy, I replaced milk in my coffee with coconut cream; tried tofu and soy sour cream instead of their conventional, animal-based alternatives.

If you can't say no to dairy completely, at least make better choices about what types of dairy you consume and where it's sourced. If you have to eat dairy, organic and fermented choices are preferred.

LONGEVITY DIET PRINCIPLE 10

CONSUME COFFEE AND WINE IN MODERATION

Finally, the thing I get asked the most about health is whether it's okay to drink coffee and wine. My answer is yes. If you are going to stray from drinking water, those are the two beverages that should be your treat—

but in moderation. It's okay to have one to two espressos and one to two glasses of red wine each day, but it should be done as early as possible and with food. Both will affect the quality of your sleep. One recent study showed that two glasses of wine per day led to an 18 percent drop in the odds of early death. Meanwhile, those who drank coffee saw their odds drop by 10 percent. Another study also linked coffee to a lower risk of heart failure, stroke, and heart disease. Neither drink should be the core of what you consume in your diet, but a little of each won't hurt you.

In the next section, we'll dig far more into the specifics of what different foods and drinks bring to the table as you overhaul your eating habits.

CHAPTER 4

FOODS TO EAT FOR LONGEVITY

If you remember one thing from this book, it should be the importance of eating whole plants. When in doubt, reach for something green that was grown in the ground. For those of us who grew up with a food pyramid guiding our choices, think of fruits and vegetables as the base. I already mentioned that organic farm-grown meat is good in smaller quantities, while organic wild fish can be a part of your diet in larger quantities. We'll leave it at that, it's pretty straightforward. For your convenience, I've put together a shopping list with longevity-focused products. Have a look before you next go grocery shopping.

As I outline specific foods to incorporate into your diet, I'm going to spend the most time on plants. I'll go through 14 fruits, vegetables, legumes, nuts and seeds, listed in alphabetical order, and explain why they contribute to living a longer, healthier life. This list isn't exhaustive, of course. But these foods should add some color and detail to the principles I outlined already. They should be part of your daily routine.

Download infographic here:
sergeyyoung.com/longevity-diet-shopping-list

Sergey Young

LONGEVITY SHOPPING LIST

1. CRUCIFEROUS VEGETABLES
- [ ] Broccoli
- [ ] Brussels Sprouts
- [ ] Cabbage

2. ROOT VEGETABLES
- [ ] Sweet potatoes
- [ ] Beets
- [ ] Carrots

3. LEAFY VEGETABLES AND SALADS
- [ ] Spinach
- [ ] Kale
- [ ] Chard

4. NIGHTSHADES
- [ ] Eggplants
- [ ] Peppers
- [ ] Tomatoes

5. LEGUMES
- [ ] Beans
- [ ] Peas
- [ ] Lentils

6. CITRUS FRUITS
- [ ] Lemons
- [ ] Limes
- [ ] Grapefruits

7. GARLIC AND ONIONS
- [ ] Shallots
- [ ] Yellow / Red onions
- [ ] Garlic

8. FRESH HERBS & SPICES
- [ ] Parsley
- [ ] Coriander
- [ ] Ginger

9. BERRIES
- [ ] Blackberries
- [ ] Blueberries
- [ ] Raspberries

10. ORGANIC MEAT AND POULTRY

11. TREE NUTS & SEEDS
- [ ] Tree nuts
- [ ] Chia seeds
- [ ] Sesame seeds

12. WILD FISH AND SEAFOOD
- [ ] Salmon
- [ ] Cod
- [ ] Shrimp

13. HEALTHY FATS
- [ ] Olive oil
- [ ] Flaxseed oil
- [ ] Avocado

14. MISCELLANEOUS
- [ ] Eggs
- [ ] Plant milk
- [ ] Fermented food
- [ ] Mushrooms

Some suggestions, list is not complete

Connect with me on:

Website: sergeyyoung.com

Facebook: sergeyyoung200

Linkedin: Sergey Young

DOWNLOAD THIS INFOGRAPHIC HERE: WWW.SERGEYYOUNG.COM/INFOGRAPHICS

That's the key here: routine. It doesn't help to make a spinach smoothie and smother your salad with olive oil for just a day or two, then go back to old habits and processed meals. The key is to create a lifestyle, which also means finding or creating a healthy community, in which longevity-centric choices become the default. To put it another way, these foods should become extremely familiar menu items. That said, a single sweet potato could very well be the first step on the road to such a healthy lifestyle. Start small if you have to, but remember: the more plants, the better.

AVOCADOS

Tattooed on celebrities, travelled with and smeared on toast, these guys are deserving of all their hype. Avocados aid in antioxidant absorption from other vegetables, many of which help fight cancer. Fiber, which does everything from lower cholesterol to control weight, has been linked to longer life spans and—you guessed it—avocados are packed full of it (about 11 percent of the daily value!). Avocados also help prevent metabolic syndrome, a condition that leads to an increased risk of cardiovascular diseases like heart disease and stroke—again, the leading causes of death worldwide. Avocado is a very good source of healthy fats that have anti-inflammatory properties, meaning they are good in the battle against Alzheimer's, cancer, and more. Avocado is a usual suspect in my lunch as a side to basically everything.

Miranda Kerr is a long-time advocate for avocados, which are a good source of vitamins, minerals, and healthy fats. Kerr told Health Alkaline that she often makes hearty dinner salads using nutrient-packed avocado, feta, and spinach.

ARTICHOKES

This plant brings us back to the Mediterranean, the epicenter of our healthy living goals. Artichokes are the buds of a purple flower that, in some cases, can grow to be over three feet tall. While they're native to the Mediterranean, I recommend putting some on your plate no matter where you are. On the USDA's list of antioxidant-rich foods, artichokes are number seven. Artichokes are also anti-inflammatory, which is important for longevity, particularly after the 100-year mark. Inflammation is the root cause of countless diseases of the mind and body, including diabetes, cancer and cognitive decline. Artichokes are also packed with flavonoids, which also help reduce the risk of dying early.

The Californian town of Castroville, located 19 miles northeast of Monterey, is nicknamed "the Artichoke Capital of the World", and is home to a major producer of artichokes. Due to the favorable Californian climate, artichokes are available throughout the year.

My favorite dish combines three items from this longevity food list is artichokes roasted with garlic and sprinkled with cold pressed olive oil. Easy, healthy, delicious!

BLUEBERRIES

We've already mentioned that heart disease is the leading killer in the world—but did we mention that blueberries are linked with better heart health? One researcher gathered data from over 93,000 young women. Because young women are at a low risk of heart attack, it was easier to figure out what factors increased their risk. The findings were simple and delicious: the less blueberries and strawberries women ate, the higher the risk.

Flavonoids are plant compounds that often have a powerful antioxidant effect. A type of flavonoid called anthocyanin is responsible for the blueberry's color and gives blueberries many of their health benefits.

Toss blueberries into a smoothie for breakfast or grab a handful as a snack, as long as you routinely get them on your plate.

BROCCOLI & CAULIFLOWER

According to a large Chinese study, adults who ate the most cruciferous vegetables had a 22 percent reduced risk of dying from any cause. That's nothing to scoff at. So, what other cruciferous vegetables should be on your plate? Broccoli and cauliflower. Broccoli has many of the same benefits as spinach. Indeed, many vegetables overlap in the ways they can improve your life quality and span. Broccoli is packed with fiber—with nearly 1 gram of fiber per 10 calories—and helps prevent stomach and intestinal cancers.

Cauliflower has burst onto the foodie scene in recent years, with many people using it as a low-carb substitute for everything from rice to pizza crust. Indeed, cauliflower is quite the upgrade from such processed foods—particularly from a longevity perspective. Broccoli and cauliflower both contain something called sulforaphane, which can activate an anti-aging pathway called Nrf2. But don't forget our principles when it comes to cauliflower. Try to buy fresh, local, organic cauliflower and don't be fooled by things like cauliflower pizza crust that are in fact heavily processed.

I suggest you also try other vegetables from the cruciferous family: broccolini, white and red cabbage, Chinese cabbage, Romanesco, Brussels sprouts, bok choy, kohlrabi. There are countless ways you can incorporate them into your diet: baked and roasted with spices, pureed, and as a soup ingredient to name a few.

CARROTS

It has been said that the creator of Apple, Steve Jobs, would sometimes only eat carrots for weeks at a time, turning his skin almost orange at times! I wouldn't recommend following in the Apple founder's footsteps when it comes to that level of carrot consumption, but I would suggest working them into your diet. Research shows that carrots contain substances that slow down the rate of aging—precisely the aim of these food recommendations. People who never eat fruits and vegetables die an average of three years before those who consume copious amounts of them, carrots included.

Carrots are a great side dish, especially when they're local and organic. Just roast them in the oven with spices of your choice and you will get an amazing side dish to accompany any meat, poultry or fish. My kids love carrots and we make sure to take full advantage of this by regularly cooking carrot soups, shredding raw baby carrots in their salads, and packing carrot sticks in school lunch boxes.

FERMENTED FOODS

One study at the University of Idaho found that many people who live past 100 eat fermented foods daily. I recommend kimchi as the place to start. It's fermented cabbage with spices like garlic, salt, and vinegar. Kimchi contains vitamins A, B, and C. As with all fermented foods, it also comes packed with healthy probiotics, which are the crux of the immune system. If you're in the market for a new hobby, you could of course ferment and spice some cabbage yourself, but I prefer to grab a can from a local store.

Kombucha is another fermented product I recommend. You can easily cook it at home, but if you choose to buy it in a store, make sure the list of ingredients is healthy. A host of celebrities like Lady Gaga, Zoe Kravitz, Kourtney Kardashian, Gwyneth Paltrow and Halle Berry are currently obsessed with this probiotic-packed fermented drink.

LEGUMES

Next up, we have legumes—chickpeas, peas, beans, and lentils—which should be another staple of your diet, as they are staples of the longevity-extending Mediterranean and Japanese diets already helping people.

One study found that legumes are in fact the most important predictor of survival in people aged 70 and over from around the world. They are also full of something called polyphenols, which protect against heart disease and cancer. Eat them in conjunction with lots of fruits and veggies, and you'll be fighting major killers from every direction.

Kate Hudson mixes beans and lentils into her diet regularly, pairing them with salads, rice, fish, and a wide array of veggie dishes. As the face of her own fitness-fashion line, she's got to stay fit, and wholesome foods like these help her do just that.

NUTS

While I don't recommend snacking continuously throughout the day, per our earlier principle about intermittent fasting, a handful of nuts are great if you simply must be on-the-go, or just need a little extra food in your stomach. I recommend walnuts and almonds. Almonds fend off insulin resistance and walnuts clear your arteries. A Harvard study of 120,000 people found that those who eat nuts daily live longer than those who don't. Nuts have been shown to help with healthy cholesterol levels and lower blood pressure, in addition to many of the anti-carcinogenic and anti-inflammation effects cited with veggies. Plus, nuts are easy to stock up on and require no preparation. You can easily store them in your office, purse or car glove compartment.

"Raw almonds are the perfect snack. A handful can hold me over to my next meal. Better yet, they are so good for you," Heidi Klum said in an interview with Shape.

ONION AND GARLIC

While tomatoes can be a great topping to any salad, onion and garlic can be a great flavor base to any dish—and, of course, to improved health. Both are members of the *Allium* genus, which means they contain countless important vitamins and minerals. Throughout human history, garlic has been used to treat diseases, while spring onions have folate and lutein, which can help with memory. Garlic and onions are also pre-biotics that promote good gut health and help control blood sugar. Plus, they contain compounds that are anti-carcinogenic and help reduce the risk of heart disease. These two are practically basics; it's always helpful to have them on hand.

FUN FACT: do you know that the name "Chicago" is the French version of the Miami-Illinois word *shikaakwa* ("Stinky Onion"), named for the garlic plant (not onion) *Allium* tricoccum common along the Chicago River. It's a great reason for the citizens of the third biggest city in the U.S. to add garlic to their diet.

Cameron Diaz, actress and bestselling author of *The Longevity Book: The Science of Aging, the Biology of Strength, and the Privilege of Time*, has extensively researched the connection between longevity and nutrition. Cameron has a lot of ideas about food that I can relate to. One of them is that lemon, garlic, olive oil and salt can make anything taste good. Garlic can be a part of literally every dish. Add minced garlic while roasting root vegetables, when marinating chicken, to enhance a soup flavor, and as an important ingredient to homemade dips like hummus or eggplant.

Don't forget that there are several types of onion. Use fresh stalks of scallions, chives and spring onions, and bulbs of yellow, white, sweet and red onions and shallots. Add them to your salads, stews, stir fries, and soups.

PUMPKIN

Pumpkin might seem like a Halloween decoration more than a staple of longevity, but in reality it's both! Pumpkins, like carrots, contain large amounts of beta-carotene, a powerful antioxidant. Pumpkin is packed full of potassium, with more milligrams per cup than most fruits and vegetables. Less than two percent of Americans consume enough potassium. Doing so reduces the risk of mortality by 20 percent overall. As if that's not enough, increasing how much potassium you consume while decreasing sodium levels has been shown to lower the risk of ischemic heart disease by a whopping 49 percent.

I am not a big fan of pumpkin, but it turns out there are plenty of delicious ways to cook them. And I am not talking about pumpkin pie! Try baked spicy pumpkin or curry winter pumpkin soup.

SEEDS

GI stands for glycemic index, which ranks foods by how they affect blood glucose levels. Eating low-GI foods prevents blood sugar spikes, in turn helping to fend off things like diabetes and cardiovascular disease. Eating refined grains and starches has been associated with weight gain and other health concerns. But grains with a low GI value? Good to go. The two I recommend are buckwheat and quinoa. Both are technically seeds. Buckwheat is a great source of fiber, which is good for heart health, while quinoa has been linked to a substantial decrease in the risk of premature death.

Cooked quinoa is one of my favorite salad ingredients and cooked buckwheat is a base for my morning bowl of "whole grain", berries and nuts.

SPINACH

What do Spice Girl Victoria Beckham and cartoon sailor Popeye have in common? They both eat a lot of spinach, according to the tabloids (or, in Popeye's case, the television). I'm not going to tell you to take things that far, but spinach should definitely play a prominent role in your longevity diet. I recommend eating spinach or other leafy green vegetables like kale and chard daily. The darker the green, the better. Plants, and green vegetables in particular, stave off deadly disease and contain far fewer calories than any meat, as already mentioned. They also contain countless essential vitamins and antioxidants that neutralize free radicals and thus help to prevent cancer.

I prefer spinach in a raw form rather than cooked, so I add spinach to my morning smoothie and use it as a base to my salads.

SWEET POTATO

One American centenarian named Leslie Brown ate a sweet potato a day until she was 100 years old. Elsewhere, among the residents of the Japanese island of Okinawa are plenty of people living past 100. Sweet potatoes are a staple of the Okinawan diet, providing good part of their daily calories. Consuming this amount of sweet potato also creates a carb-to-protein ratio associated with long life spans in animals. More broadly, the benefits of sweet potatoes echo the benefits of many of the fruits and vegetables on this list: fiber, vitamins, minerals, and more. The easiest way to add them to your diet is to replace regular potatoes with sweet ones: puree, add to your soups, or even "French fry" them.

TOMATOES

The Mediterranean diet, once again, has been shown time and time again to promote a long life span and improve health along the way, including lowering death rates from heart disease and cancer. Tomatoes are an important part of the Mediterranean diet. Tomatoes contain countless antioxidants like beta-carotene and important vitamins E and C. According to a U.S. Department of Agriculture report *What We Eat In America*, one-third of us don't get enough vitamin C in our diets. People who do have enough vitamin C in their diets have a 25 percent lower chance of death by any cause.

My favorite way to consume fresh tomatoes is a version of a garden salad with olive oil dressing. I eat it often. I also like Spanish cold tomato soup Gazpacho in summer and a hot spicy tomato soup on a colder day.

CHAPTER 5
LONGEVITY TOXINS

Between our longevity principles and a pretty substantial longevity grocery list, you should already have a good idea of what foods to avoid. If you're adding in plants, olive oil, and other nutritious staples, there's little to no room for bad stuff anyway. Still, I wanted to spell it out explicitly. Certain foods are straight-up longevity killers and should be avoided at all costs. In this section, I'll keep it simple. I've organized these five categories of longevity toxins into three buckets of food and drink that should set off alarm bells no matter what. Sugary drinks, processed foods, and condiments might seem harmless in small doses, but they lurk at the root of myriad deadly diseases. Let's take a closer look.

This simple infographic can help you stay away from the dangerous foods. Print it out and stick it to your fridge.

Download infographic here:
sergeyyoung.com/5-longevity-toxins

Sergey Young

5 LONGEVITY TOXINS

1 SUGARY DRINKS

- soft drinks
- energy drinks
- fruit juices

 6X a glass of apple juice = 6 tsp. of sugar

 10X a can of soda ≈ 10 tsp. of sugar

 8X a can of energy drink ≈ 8 tsp. of sugar

2 FAST FOODS

- burgers and fries
- chicken nuggets
- pizzas

ARE LOADED WITH:

- sodium
- unhealthy fats
- sweeteners

AND:

- have minimal nutritional value

3 PROCESSED FOODS

- deli meats, bacon, sausages
- breakfast cereals
- flavored yogurts
- frozen dinners, canned soups

ARE LOADED WITH:

 artificial colors, preservatives, nitrates

 sodium

 sweeteners

AND:

+500 add on average 500 extra calories per day

1 TABLESPOON OF

1X ketchup = 1 tsp. of sugar

+80 Caesar salad dressing ≈ 80 calories

260X Italian dressing ≈ 260 mg of sodium

4 SAUCES

- store-bought sauces and condiments
- manufactured salad dressings and marinades

5 WHEAT PRODUCTS

- bread, bagels
- cookies, pastry
- «white» pasta

 have low nutritional value

 spike blood sugar

can contribute to obesity and heart disease

Connect with me on:

Website: sergeyyoung.com

Facebook: sergeyyoung200

Linkedin: Sergey Young

SUGARY DRINKS

Sometimes, we focus so much on what food we're piling on our plates that we forget to consider the beverages we're drinking alongside them. Far too often, the beverages we choose are packed with sugar, which is detrimental to health and longevity. That's why developing a healthy hydration habit—aka drinking plenty of water—is so crucial to long-term health. Besides immediate benefits, water will also replace these hidden longevity killers in your diet. Indeed, Harvard researcher Vasanti Malik doesn't mince words: the optimal intake of sugary drinks is precisely zero.

Sugary drinks have been linked to 184,000 deaths worldwide each year, the majority from diabetes. I'm not just talking about soda, although Americans consume billions of gallons of soft drinks annually, despite well-documented health concerns such as an increased risk of stroke. Fruit drinks and sports drinks often contain even more sugar, yet people are fooled by the "fruit" and "sports" in their names. Cranberry juice has 12 teaspoons of sugar in a 12-ounce serving—two more than a standard soda—for example. Some coffee drinks from popular coffee chains are packed with hidden sugar too; an Iced Caramel Macchiato alone has 34 grams.

High sugar consumption has been linked to a long list of negative health effects that lead to premature death, as already mentioned. Of the 24 teaspoons of added sugar that adult men consume daily, over half come from drinks: 42 percent from soft, energy, and sports drinks, with another 9 percent from fruit drinks. Over the last five decades, there's been a 500 percent increase in consumption of such beverages. In a study of over 450,000 people from 10 European countries, greater consumption of sweet drinks was associated with a higher risk of all-cause mortality. Another study broke it down even more: drinking just two or more sweet drinks daily increases the risk of early death by an enormous 63 percent for women. Moderation is not a practical route for sugary drinks either, as the sugar lights up reward pathways that will leave you wanting more. Simply stay away!

FAST AND PROCESSED FOODS

This category is broad but important. Fast food and processed food might shrink your life span and health span as well—dramatically. Arguably, eating fast and processed foods may kill more people than smoking. And a 50-year study showed that together, an unhealthy lifestyle, poor diet, and smoking can reduce your life span by an eye-popping 23 years. Joel Fuhrman, MD calls it a "fast food genocide".

When I say fast food, I mean anything that's readily available and doesn't have to be prepared, whether your stereotypical burger and fries from a drive-thru, a frozen meal, or even a granola bar. This food is often popular for the convenience it offers, but that convenience isn't worth your health. Having fast food at least once a week increases your risk of diabetes, while having it at least twice a week ups the chances of metabolic syndrome, type 2 diabetes, and death from heart disease.

Fast food in the traditional sense of the word is also heavily, heavily processed. And to extend longevity, you should in fact avoid all processed foods. Remember, buy close to the source and eat foods whole as much as possible, and this will be taken care of. Processed foods are packed with calories, palm oil, preservatives, chemicals, and synthetic ingredients. They're also low in nutrients. That's why processed foods cause weight gain and obesity, which is linked to many cancers, per the World Cancer Research Fund.

In case it's not already clear, excess calories will shorten your life span; 50 excess calories per day over a 10-year period packs on 50 pounds that increase your risk of chronic illness and cancer. Processed foods are also full of salt that, in conjunction with unhealthy fat and added sugar, creates cravings—if not addiction—again throwing any idealistic talk of moderation out the window.

Another important issue with processed foods that I must mention is that they may contain generally recognized as safe (GRAS) ingredients. GRAS ingredients may be found in many processed foods—from cereals and frozen dinners to salad dressings and snacks. The FDA has made a permanent rule that allows food companies to add new ingredients to the food supply with almost no federal oversight. According to *Consumer Reports* there are an estimated 1,000 GRAS substances for which safety decisions were made by the food industry without any notice at all to FDA. Some GRAS-designated substances, like artificial sweeteners and MSG are controversial and have been the subject of public criticism for years. For example, trans fat used to be a member of the GRAS ingredients list until 2018 when the World Health Organization introduced a 6-step guide to eliminate industrially-produced trans-fatty acids from the global food supply. The reason it happened was a number of studies that suggested that consuming trans-fatty acids may increase risk of some types of cancer. This story illustrates that not all GRAS ingredients are safe for consumers.

When I say processed foods, that includes foods like bread and pasta that are only edible because they've been heavily refined. When you go out to eat, say no to the bread and butter for this reason.

In a paper, Doctor Fuhrman notes that the calories from 200 grams of white bread enter your bloodstream within five to ten minutes, whereas those from 200 grams of beans enter over the course of hours. The latter is dramatically better for you because you don't get the same insulin spike. Insulin, for the record, inhibits a protein called SKN-1 that increases your life span, in addition to a protein that's important for tumor suppression and stem cell maintenance. But you don't have to remember all of that. Studies suggest, if it's processed, you should pass.

CONDIMENTS

Coffee chains aren't just sneaky when it comes to sugar in drinks. Once, I went to a coffee shop and bought a pretty healthy salad. Lots of green and little that was processed. In all, the salad was only 100 or so calories, and packed full of nutrients. But the dressing? It contained more calories than the salad itself and the list of ingredients had several suspicious items!

Many people clean up their diets yet don't realize they're still consuming common longevity toxins—like added sugar and unhealthy fats—because of the sauces they put on top of a seemingly healthy lunch or dinner. Common condiments are full of coloring, artificial flavors, salt, sugar, and other things that will hinder your health span and life span. It's best to avoid them.

If you've defined your relationship with dairy as avoiding it altogether, that will take care of things like Caesar salad dressing and ranch dressing, which are high-calorie meal toppers. But you're still not in the clear with other condiments. One teaspoon of ketchup is the same as downing a packet of sugar. Barbecue sauce tends to come with at least 10 grams of sugar per two teaspoons—and most of us pile on far more than that. Fat-free dressing may seem healthy at first glance, but sugar is usually added to it too.

Following our earlier longevity diet principles, you should turn to olive oil, avocado oil, flaxseed oil or other healthy cold pressed oils instead. You can easily cook healthy versions of mayonnaise, tahini, peso and other dressings at home. This way you will control the ingredients' quality and keep your menu simple and your body healthier.

CHAPTER 6

SUPPLEMENTS

Building good eating habits is of utmost importance for anyone looking to extend their life spans. Hopefully, the principles and tools outlined thus far will set you on the right path. But I know the tough reality: no one is perfect, and the modern diet isn't either. It may not be possible to always buy wild fish or local vegetables, which contain more of the nutrients your body needs. Indeed, nutrient deficiencies are extremely common in the United States. Additionally, caloric restriction—once again linked to longevity—may leave you feeling like you have to choose between certain superfoods. But you don't. Supplements are a great way to make up for small deficiencies in your diet, in turn protecting against aging and disease.

It is very important to understand that there is no miracle pill or multivitamin supplement that will work for everyone. Before stocking up on vitamins and minerals, you must visit your family doctor to discuss your lifestyle and take a close look at your blood test results. A quick trip to your local CVS or Walgreens won't help. Taking over-the-counter supplements could be a waste of your time and money, or even dangerous.

Some specific supplements can jump-start your journey to 100 years or more, but for them to do so you must choose the products and the dose together with your doctor.

It is very important to understand that there is no miracle pill or multivitamin supplement that will work for everyone. Before stocking up on vitamins and minerals, you must visit your family doctor to discuss your lifestyle and take a close look at your blood test results

Sergey Young

10 LONGEVITY SUPPLEMENTS

1 VITAMIN D3

Vitamin D is essential for several reasons, including maintaining healthy bones and teeth

HELPS

- support immune and nervous system health
- regulate insulin levels

2 OMEGA 3

- contains essential fatty acids
- strengthens the vascular system
- reduces cholesterol

3 MILK THISTLE

Milk thistle has been shown to possess antioxidant and anti-inflammatory properties. It supports liver and bone health

4 SEAWEED

Supports thyroid function and helps to detox

6 GINKGO BILOBA

Reduces inflammation and helps improve cognitive function

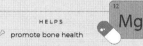

5 NAD+ BOOSTER

Makes sirtuin proteins work, i.e. protects cells from age-related decline; improves memory

7 FIBER

Studies suggest that increasing your dietary fiber intake is associated with a reduced risk of dying from cardiovascular disease and all cancers

HELPS

- promote digestive health
- control blood sugar levels
- manage healthy weight

8 MAGNESIUM

Aging is often associated with chronic magnesium deficiency

HELPS

- promote bone health
- lower risk of type 2 diabetes
- improve cardiovascular health

9 GARLIC CONCENTRATE

Be aware that modern processing methods preserve the benefits of garlic while reducing the odor

HELPS

- improve cardiovascular health
- fight fungal and microbial infections

10 GREEN POWDER

Boosts the immune system, reduces inflammation and detoxifies the body

WARNING: CONSULT WITH YOUR DOCTOR BEFORE TAKING ANY SUPPLEMENTS

Connect with me on:

Website:
sergeyyoung.com

Facebook:
sergeyyoung200

Linkedin:
Sergey Young

DOWNLOAD THIS INFOGRAPHIC HERE: WWW.SERGEYYOUNG.COM/INFOGRAPHICS

In the rest of this chapter, I'll run through the supplements I've taken at some point in my life. I always rotate and change them according to my blood test results. Here is another visual aid for you: a top 10 list of longevity supplements that you can consider together with your doctor.

OMEGA-3

Download infographic here:
sergeyyoung.com/10-longevity-supplements

I've already said that you should opt for fish over meat the majority of the time, in part because of sourcing and in part because fish is full of omega-3 fatty acids. EPA and DHA are primarily found in fish, while ALA (another omega-3 fatty acid) is in seeds and nuts. Harvard research has shown that by increasing your levels of all three fatty acids, you have a 35 percent lower risk of death by heart disease. In that study, which was based on 16 years of data on 2,700 adults aged 65 or older, people weren't using omega-3 fatty acid supplements. But you should be. Only 10 percent of Americans regularly take the supplement, even though it reduces triglycerides and inflammation, fights against Alzheimer's, reduces the risk of fatty liver disease, and might reduce the risk of developing some types of cancer.

Still don't believe me? A study of over 25,000 healthy adults showed that a moderate dose of omega-3 decreased the chance of a heart attack. The only group it didn't reduce risk for? Those who ate too little fish. The takeaway: get a good baseline of omega-3 in your diet, then toss in a supplement for the added benefits.

VITAMIN D3

Next up, I recommend taking a look at vitamin D3. One meta study showed that elderly women who take a daily dose live longer than those who don't. Other research suggests similar longevity benefits: if you're deficient in the major form of vitamin D (called 25-hydroxyvitamin D), you have an increased risk of age-related disease, from Alzheimer's to cancer. A few studies have found that people with low levels of vitamin D in their blood indeed die sooner.

Just as omega-3 is best gotten from fish and food, vitamin D is best gotten from sunlight. But in addition to getting outside and getting moving, it's useful to supplement—particularly in dark winter months.

SEAWEED

Seaweed is a super-supplement and should definitely be in your rotation. Let's start with the basics: seaweed is packed with antioxidants which, as already mentioned, prevent inflammation—a chronic problem lurking at the root of everything from obesity to arthritis. But also, seaweed is packed full of iodine, which is crucial for your thyroid but largely missing from the modern diet. And it will provide your body with even more omega-3 fatty acids!

Nori, which you might be familiar with from sushi hand rolls, and spirulina are two types of seaweed that come in powdered forms, perfect for smoothies or other drinks. The benefits keep stacking up, too. One rare form of seaweed has shown potential to lower blood pressure. Seaweed also contains something called fucoxanthin. You don't have to

Spirulina is a type of seaweed that come in powdered form, perfect for smoothies or other drinks!

know how to pronounce it; just know that it reduces the accumulation of fat. Last but not least, seaweed is packed full of vitamins A, B, and C.

GINKGO BILOBA

I'll be honest: if you had told me to consume ginkgo biloba a few years ago, I would have looked at you like you had three heads. "Ginkgo who?" But now that I've done some research, I can't imagine going without it. Ginkgo biloba, if you're unfamiliar, is often called a "living fossil." It's the world's oldest living plant, dating back hundreds of millions of years. Basically, the species—and the individual plants themselves—knows a little something about longevity.

But will it help with your longevity? It sure will—which is why it's already one of the 10 most popular dietary supplements sold stateside. The gingko nut was first identified as a treatment for lung diseases, but clinical research on the power of its leaf extract with regard to cardiovascular diseases began in the 1960s. If you remember one thing about this living fossil, remember this: its extract has since been shown to help mammals resist stress, improve cognition, and live longer. It can also alleviate high cholesterol levels and high blood pressure.

MILK THISTLE

Milk thistle is a flowering herb—or, as I like to put it, a super herb and another supplement that should be on your shopping list. It's the most researched plant for the treatment of liver disease and can also help fight cirrhosis and gallbladder disorder. Plus, milk thistle contains a plant compound called silymarin that's anti-inflammatory and an antioxidant, reducing free radical production (again, free radicals are linked to cancer).

It's been shown to help people with diabetes improve insulin resistance and lower their bad cholesterol. It also has more direct anti-aging effects. And once again, aging is at the root of many of the diseases we've mentioned thus far. Milk thistle can be found as a capsule, powder, or liquid extract.

NAD+ BOOSTER

NAD+ booster is another supplement that may be new to you. NAD stands for nicotinamide adenine dinucleotide and is a coenzyme, present in all cells of the body, that turns all the healthy things you eat into energy. While its natural levels are boosted by intermittent fasting, I recommend taking NAD+ booster in capsule form as well.

It's been suggested that NAD+ depletion plays a "major role in the aging process," which once again is what we are aiming to fight. That's because NAD+ also makes your sirtuin proteins work—proteins that, in a nutshell, protect your cells from age-related decline... so much so that they've been dubbed "guardians of the genome." Sirtuin levels tend to decrease with age. Supplementing with NAD+ booster can help offset this and is particularly useful for fending off neurodegenerative disease.

FIBER

A key principle of a longevity diet is focusing on plants, in part because they are packed with fiber. I recommend doubling down on that approach by also taking a fiber supplement. This should never be mistaken as a substitute for vegetables. But a diet high in fiber, once again, protects against chronic disease and extends your life span, so why not add in some rice bran or apple fiber? More specifically, a 10-gram increase in dietary fiber has been shown to cause a 10 percent drop in the risk of dying from any cause.

GREENS POWDER

Greens powders are dietary supplements that you can add to any drink. Mixing in 10 grams of greens powder has been shown to decrease oxidative damage by 30 percent and lower blood pressure. Many greens powders also have things like pre- and probiotics added, which can improve your gut health—the core of the immune system. Working all these supplements into your routine is like putting an extra fence around an already well-built house.

MAGNESIUM

Aging is frequently associated with chronic magnesium deficiency. Magnesium is an essential cofactor for numerous biological processes and is a critical factor for normal cellular and body homeostasis. Over the past years, the impact of magnesium on molecular and physiological processes of aging and on age-related diseases has been researched extensively. Unfortunately, many people are deficient in this essential mineral and require magnesium supplementation. As with other supplements consult your doctor before deciding if you need it.

GARLIC CONCENTRATE

Garlic has been traditionally used for cardiovascular health. It is also believed to be very efficient in supporting the immune system, cellular detoxification and enhancing the body's response to oxidative stress. Don't worry about this supplement destroying your fresh breath and annihilating your social life – modern processing methods preserve the natural goodness of garlic while eliminating the strong odor.

**Building and
maintaining healthy habits
is an issue of lifestyle, not
just grocery shopping**

CHAPTER 7

A CASE STUDY

I hope that outlining diet principles, listing foods to eat and avoid, and tossing in some supplements is enough to push you firmly in the direction of your 100th birthday. But I wanted to end this book by returning to a point made at the beginning: sometimes, simply having access to information about health isn't enough. If that were the case, we'd all be living to 100 already. Instead, digesting longevity information and putting it into practice is what trips a lot of us up. That's because building and maintaining healthy habits is an issue of lifestyle, not just grocery shopping. To drive this point home, I thought it might be worth taking a closer look at my story and how my family and I implement the principles I've outlined.

EAT FROM THE OCEAN

In the last section, I mentioned two supplements that can help you live longer: omega-3 fatty acids and seaweed. In my family, we get plenty of both by eating a very ocean-centric diet. Being born in a city on the Pacific Ocean and having spent the first 17 years of my life by the coast, I feel very comfortable with the idea of eating from the sea. Now, we consume around three servings of fish per week. We avoid farmed-raised fish.

We buy only wild small-sized fish, that contain less mercury. We love sardines, anchovies, herring, mackerel icefish, wild salmon and sole. Kids often eat fish soups; adults opt for roasted or baked fish with herbs and garlic.

By emphasizing foods from the ocean, we get plenty of omega-3 fatty acids. Once again, omega-3 is crucial to preventing heart disease, the number one killer in the world.

LOVE OUR VEGGIES

The very first principle of a longevity diet, though, is making sure plants represent the bulk of what's on your plate. In my family, we do just that, again echoing the advice of numerous food experts. D. Craig Willcox, PhD, who co-wrote The Okinawa Program, suggests readers eat as far down the food chain as they can, which of course means consuming more plants. If I had to briefly describe my family diet, I would call it heavily plant-based.

However, for us, the diet staple isn't grains, bread or potatoes, as is the case in many Western diets. Instead, it's the sweet potato, which is packed full of essential vitamins and minerals without being packed full of calories, and a variety of cruciferous vegetables. We love all types of cruciferous vegetables, but Brussels sprouts and broccoli are among our favorites. We stir-fry them with garlic and a splash of tamari or steam them with lemon juice and olive oil.

Our kids need additional motivation, like most kids do, to eat vegetables on a regular basis, so we use a carrot-and-stick approach. We try to add a whole plant garnish to each meal and add green leafy vegetables to their smoothies. Unfortunately for the kids, we have a "no sugar/no sweets" policy at home. Speaking of kids, here is another list that will help you set up your kids for longevity.

Download infographic here:
sergeyyoung.com/10-longevity-tips-for-kids

Sergey Young

10 LONGEVITY TIPS FOR KIDS

-10 YEARS

1 DON'T SMOKE

Instill in your kids the knowledge that smoking or doing drugs is dangerous

2 DRINK WATER

Avoid sugary drinks to set a good example to your kids and teach them to drink more water

3 BEFRIEND A DOCTOR

Take your kids to a family doctor on a regular basis for check-ups

4 LEARN TO COOK HEALTHY

Feed your kids plant-based meals and organic meat and poultry. Teach them to cook their own food and why homemade meals are healthier than fast and processed foods

5 MOVE DAILY

Accustom your kids to regular physical activity, teach them different types of exercises: yoga, cardio and resistance training. Bond with your kids on daily walks and regular hikes

6 LIMIT USE OF GADGETS

Limit entertainment use of technological gadgets to 20 min per day. Encourage kids to read paper books

7 MEDITATE

Introduce your kids to meditation techniques and encourage them to get into the habit of doing it every day. Start with a simple breathing meditation

8 BE KIND AND GRATEFUL

Teach your kids the importance of being kind to others and grateful for what they have

SAFETY FIRST

9 BE SOCIAL

Help your kids to discover the value of friendship and community support

10 STAY SAFE

Explain to your kids the importance of making good choices regarding general safety: responsible driving, hygiene, social distancing when needed. And no extreme sports, please :)

Connect with me on:

Website:
sergeyyoung.com

 Facebook:
sergeyyoung200

 Linkedin:
Sergey Young

DOWNLOAD THIS INFOGRAPHIC HERE: WWW.SERGEYYOUNG.COM/INFOGRAPHICS

STICK TO SMALL PLATES

An important rule we follow in our household, taught by Confucious, is eat until you're 80 percent full—a rule many of us would do well to follow. It has been shown that bigger plates and spoons lead to bigger portions and this means you eat more. In a study conducted by Brian Wansink, Koert van Ittersum, and James E. Painter, they concluded that "because people eat most of what they serve themselves, any contextual cues that lead them to over-serve should lead them to over-eat."

Very often food becomes associated with your social life, or serves to cope with trauma or stress, or is used to "treat yourself." Thus, overindulging gets confused or repackaged as self-care.

Really, we should eat to nourish ourselves, and nourishment actually comes from exhibiting some good old-fashioned self-control. Caloric restriction has been called "the most robust intervention for slowing aging." By eating until we are 80 percent full with the help of smaller plates, we communicate the same principle far more accessibly.

In addition to a daily habit of eating less, my wife and I fast for 36 hours each week. We start our weekly, 36-hour fasting on Monday evening, and until Wednesday morning we only drink water and herbal tea.

WALKING, HIKING, BIKING

Walking and hiking are perfect examples of things we can easily incorporate into our daily routines. There's no cost hurdle to taking a few more laps around the block. Yet many of us fail to do so. In my family, though, walking, biking, and hiking are part of our lifestyle.

Walk briskly for just 25 minutes a day and it could add seven years to your life! Walking has also been shown to have a meditative effect. In his early days at Uber, Travis Kalanick famously had a walking track on the fourth floor of the office; he'd walk around 40 hours per week. You don't necessarily need to walk that much—you don't even necessarily need 10,000 steps a day. But you do need to move your body consistently.

Try parking several blocks away from your destination or jump off public transportation a couple of stops ahead. Don't use the elevator if possible, and take your meetings outside instead of sitting in a restaurant or your office. This is what I practice daily.

ALCOHOL IN MODERATION

Alcohol consumption is also minimal in the Young household. This might seem obvious from a longevity perspective, but many people I know don't see anything counterintuitive about running in the morning, for instance, and celebrating this healthy achievement with hours of drinking in the evening. Alcohol, like coffee, should only be consumed in moderation. Our rule is to drink as little as a glass or two of wine on weekends.

SLEEP

Sleep is crucial to longevity, while short naps can help boost brain function. One study found that taking short naps, exercising regularly, and walking together bred improved "sleep health." Unfortunately, the importance of sleep is underestimated in our society.

If you can't fit in an afternoon nap because of your work schedule, at least make sure you're getting sufficient sleep at nighttime! Cutting-edge companies, though, have already realized the importance of siestas. Google is among those providing nap spaces at its offices; "no workplace is complete without a nap pod," its VP said. Recently, the New York Times even ran the article "Take Naps at Work. Apologize to No One," citing improvements in productivity and engagement. Improvement in life span is a bonus.

We don't take naps during the day, but I pay extra attention to our sleeping routine. Our bedrooms are equipped to promote healthy sleeping. There is no night light or charging devices in the bedrooms, we have blackout blinds, comfortable pillows and mattresses, and the environment is always cool (the room temperature is between 60 and 67 degrees Fahrenheit). All these conditions are required to promote good sleep quality. We also teach kids to engage in relaxing activities like reading a book before bedtime and stick to a schedule.

CHAPTER 8

CONCLUSION

For the longevity diet principles to stick in your lifestyle, you must shift your mindset and not just your eating habits. In my family, we eat healthily not because we follow a special diet, but because we believe in the principles I've described. And, most importantly, in the idea that what we put in our body every single day will impact the number of years we live and the quality of those years.

You don't need to follow my advice 100 percent if you feel it is too complicated for you right now. The changes you make should be sustainable. Learn to integrate the products I've listed in your diet in a way that is comfortable for you; ways that make you excited and happy. Try new recipes; step out of your comfort zone one change at a time. Encourage those around you, your family, your children, your spouse, and your friends to embark on this adventure alongside you. Going through lifestyle changes together will benefit everyone.

Use a 10-day Challenge list I created as a tool that helps you adapt new dietary habits and lifestyle changes.

Download infographic here: sergeyyoung.com/10-day-challenge

The whole idea behind changing your diet is the hope that it will eventually create a better existence for the years we spend on this earth, and that's what this story is all about. Keeping your body healthy keeps your brain functioning and makes your daily life immeasurably better. It is pervasive and will have a truly positive impact on all aspects of your life.

Sergey Young

10-DAY CHALLENGE

AVOID ALL ANIMAL PRODUCTS

like meat, poultry, eggs, fish and dairy. Reintroduce organic versions of these products to your diet after the 10-day period

EAT ONLY ORGANIC PLANTS

eat a variety of plants, cooked and fresh: root and cruciferous veggies, leafy greens and salads, whole grains and seeds, tree nuts, assorted beans, legumes, and peas; snack with fruits and berries

AVOID COFFEE, ALCOHOL AND THE "LONGEVITY TOXINS"

say no to sugar, processed food, fast food and products with added sweeteners

MEDITATE EVERY DAY

start with a simple breathing technique. Experiment with other types of meditation and get into the habit of doing it every day

DRINK PLENTY OF WATER

· start your day with a glass of water

· keep a bottle on your desk and take sips throughout the day

```
    1   2   3
10           4
 9           5
    8   7   6
```

WALK OUTSIDE

~ 10 000 steps a day

TRY HOMEMADE GREEN JUICES AND HERBAL TEAS

as alternative beverages to water

IMPROVE YOUR SLEEP

· go to bed at the same time every day and attempt to sleep for at least 7-8 hours

· keep your bedroom quiet, dark, and at a cooler temperature

TRY A DIGITAL DETOX

· attempt to limit your phone use to activities deemed "essential"

· switch off gadgets one hour before going to bed

USE COLD-PRESSED OILS FOR SALADS AND COOKING

like olive oil, avocado oil, flaxseed oil or coconut oil

Connect with me on:

Website:
sergeyyoung.com

 Facebook:
sergeyyoung200

 LinkedIn:
Sergey Young

DOWNLOAD THIS INFOGRAPHIC HERE: WWW.SERGEYYOUNG.COM/INFOGRAPHICS

TO KNOW MORE ABOUT
HOW YOU CAN LIVE LONGER
AND BE HEALTHIER AND HAPPIER

Sign up to my newsletter:

 SergeyYoung.com/**newsletter**

Or connect with me on Facebook and LinkedIn:

 Facebook.com/**SergeyYoung200**

Linkedin.com/in/**SergeyYoung**

REFERENCES

CHAPTER 1: INTRODUCTION

ScienceDaily. "Nearly 7 in 10 Americans are on prescription drugs." June 19, 2013. http://sciencedaily.com/releases/2013/06/130619132352.htm

CDC. Adult Obesity Facts. https://www.cdc.gov/obesity/data/adult.html

New York Times. "Eat Less Red Meat, Scientists Said. Now Some Believe That Was Bad Advice." September 30, 2019. https://www.nytimes.com/2019/09/30/health/red-meat-heart-cancer.html

The Atlantic. "How People Came to Believe Blueberries Are the Healthiest Fruit." November 15, 2017. https://www.theatlantic.com/health/archive/2017/11/blueberries/545840/

Fox News. "Latest coffee trend is to put butter in your coffee." December 15, 2014. https://www.foxnews.com/food-drink/latest-coffee-trend-is-to-put-butter-in-your-coffee

Harvard Health Publishing. "Should you try the keto diet?" October, 2018. https://www.health.harvard.edu/staying-healthy/should-you-try-the-keto-diet

Harvard Health Publishing. "Ditch the Gluten, Improve Your Health?" November 8, 2019. https://www.health.harvard.edu/staying-healthy/ditch-the-gluten-improve-your-health

CHAPTER 2: WHAT IS LONGEVITY?

ScienceDaily. "Longevity." https://www.sciencedaily.com/terms/longevity.htm

Washington University in St Louis: Institute for Public Health. "Healthspan Is More Important Than Lifespan, So Why Don't More People Know About It?" May 30, 2017. https://publichealth.wustl.edu/heatlhspan-is-more-important-than-lifespan-so-why-dont-more-people-know-about-it/

Harvard Health Publishing. "Healthy lifestyle: 5 keys to a longer life." July 5, 2018. https://www.health.harvard.edu/blog/healthy-lifestyle-5-keys-to-a-longer-life-2018070514186

World Health Organization. "The global burden of chronic diseases." https://www.who.int/nutrition/topics/2_background/en/

CNN health. "US life expectancy is still on the decline Here's why." November 26, 2019. https://edition.cnn.com/2019/11/26/health/us-life-expectancy-decline-study/index.html

HHS.gov. "Facts & Statistics: Physical Activity." https://www.hhs.gov/fitness/resource-center/facts-and-statistics/index.html#footnote-1

The Lancet. "Health and economic burden of the projected obesity trends in the USA and the UK." August 27, 2011. https://www.ncbi.nlm.nih.gov/pubmed/21872750

Moody's Analytics. "The Economic Consequences of Millennial Health." November 6, 2019. https://www.bcbs.com/sites/default/files/file-attachments/health-of-america-report/HOA-Moodys-Millennial-10-30.pdf

Brookings. "The millennial generation: A demographic bridge to America's diverse future." January, 2018. https://www.brookings.edu/research/millennials/

Scientific American. "Live Long and Proper: Genetic Factors Associated with Increased Longevity Identified." July 1, 2010. https://www.scientificamerican.com/article/genetic-factors-associated-with-increased-longevity-identified/

Kaiser Health News. "Want To Live Past 100? Centenarians Share Secrets Of Knee Bends And Nips Of Scotch." March 27, 2017. https://khn.org/news/want-to-live-past-100-centenarians-share-secrets-of-knee-bends-and-nips-of-scotch/

Wikipedia. "Centenarian." https://en.wikipedia.org/wiki/Centenarian

MashableUK. "7 companies with amazingly unique wellness programs." May 15, 2015.
https://mashable.com/2015/05/15/unique-corporate-wellness-programs/?europe=true

Monster. "7 companies with epic wellness programs."
https://www.monster.com/career-advice/article/companies-good-wellness-programs

CHAPTER 3: LONGEVITY DIET PRINCIPLES

Vox. "Why do dieters succeed or fail? The answers have little to do with food." March 13, 2018.
https://www.vox.com/science-and-health/2018/3/13/17054146/diet-isnt-working-why

Forks Over Knives. "Plant-Based on a Budget: How I Ate Well on $5 a Day." June 24, 2015.
https://www.forksoverknives.com/healthy-food-on-tight-budget/

WebMD. "7 Rules for Eating." March 23, 2009.
https://www.webmd.com/food-recipes/news/20090323/7-rules-for-eating#1

Mayo Clinic. "Meatless meals: The benefits of eating less meat." July 26, 2017.
https://www.mayoclinic.org/healthy-lifestyle/nutrition-and-healthy-eating/in-depth/meatless-meals/art-20048193

Scientific American. "The Hunger Gains: Extreme Calorie-Restriction Diet Shows Anti-Aging Results." February 16, 2017.
https://www.scientificamerican.com/article/the-hunger-gains-extreme-calorie-restriction-diet-shows-anti-aging-results/

Agus, David B. A Short Guide to a Long Life. Simon & Schuster, 2014

Everyday Health. "First Lady Michelle Obama on Healthy Eating Habits and More."
https://www.everydayhealth.com/diet-and-nutrition-pictures/first-lady-michelle-obama-on-healthy-eating-habits-and-more.aspx

Annual Review of Plant Biology. "Plants, diet, and health." April 2013. https://www.ncbi.nlm.nih.gov/pubmed/23451785

Paleohacks. "7 Amazing Foods That Cleanse Your Liver Naturally." https://blog.paleohacks.com/7-amazing-foods-that-cleanse-your-liver-naturally/

New York Times. "Blueberries May Reduce Effects of Aging." September 21, 1999. https://www.nytimes.com/1999/09/21/health/blueberries-may-reduce-effects-of-aging.html

TakePart. "Forget Saving the Planet: Being a Vegetarian Is Cheaper Than Eating Meat." October 12, 2015. http://www.takepart.com/article/2015/10/12/vegetarian-diet-savings

Harper's Bazaar. "Christie Brinkley's Exact Diet and Exercise Routine." May 28, 2019. https://www.harpersbazaar.com.au/health-fitness/christie-brinkley-diet-exercise-18060

CNN health. "Overprocessed foods add 500 calories to your diet every day, causing weight gain." May 17, 2019. https://edition.cnn.com/2019/05/17/health/ultraprocessed-foods-weight-gain-study-trnd/index.html

Live Science. "The Truth About Nitrite in Lunch Meat." May 30, 2013. https://www.livescience.com/36057-truth-nitrites-lunch-meat-preservatives.html

Agency for Toxic Substances & Disease Registry. "Nitrate/Nitrite Toxicity. What Are the Health Effects from Exposure to Nitrates and Nitrites?" December 5, 2013. https://www.atsdr.cdc.gov/csem/csem.asp?csem=28&po=10

Axe, Josh. Eat Dirt: Why Leaky Gut May Be the Root Cause of Your Health Problems and 5 Surprising Steps to Cure It. Harper Wave, 2016.

Harper's Bazaar. "Everything Cindy Crawford Does To Make 53 Look 33." June 17, 2019. https://www.harpersbazaar.com.au/health-fitness/cindy-crawford-diet-and-exercise-regime-15526

TheDiabetesCouncil.com. "Organic Foods vs Regular Conventional Food: What is the Difference?" https://www.thediabetescouncil.com/organic-foods-vs-regular-conventional-food-what-is-the-difference/

Loma Linda University: Health. "Adventist Health Study." https://adventisthealthstudy.org/?rsource=publichealth.llu.edu/adventist-health-studies/about

Mayo Clinic. "Omega-3 in fish: How eating fish helps your heart." September 28, 2019. https://www.mayoclinic.org/diseases-conditions/heart-disease/in-depth/omega-3/art-20045614

Food & Water Watch. "Factory Fish Farming." February 1, 2013. https://www.foodandwaterwatch.org/insight/factory-fish-farming

Independent.ie. "Ingesting bacteria in the soil could be crucial to health." April 5, 2014. https://www.independent.ie/lifestyle/health/ingesting-bacteria-in-the-soil-could-be-crucial-to-health-30157957.html

New York Times. "Fast Food Versus Slow Food." July 29, 2013. https://economix.blogs.nytimes.com/2013/07/29/weighing-home-cooking-and-take-out/

Harvard Health Publishing. "Eating more ultra-processed foods may shorten life span." May, 2019. https://www.health.harvard.edu/staying-healthy/eating-more-ultra-processed-foods-may-shorten-life-span

UC San Diego: Health. "Highly Processed Diets Tied to Heart Disease, Earlier Death." May 30, 2019. https://myhealth.ucsd.edu/Conditions/Heart/6,746910

The Takeout. "Fatty, high-carb foods light up your brain like drugs." June 18, 2018. https://thetakeout.com/fatty-high-carb-foods-light-up-your-brain-like-drugs-1826918195

USA Today. "Alec Baldwin: Between '30 Rock' and a 'thrilling' place." November 20, 2012. https://eu.usatoday.com/story/life/people/2012/11/19/baldwin-guardians-rock/1709087/

Healthline. "11 Proven Benefits of Olive Oil." September 14, 2018. https://www.healthline.com/nutrition/11-proven-benefits-of-olive-oil

EatingWell. "Why the Mediterranean Diet Is So Healthy." http://www.eatingwell.com/article/290484/why-the-mediterranean-diet-is-so-healthy/

The Washington Post. "Do you know how much sugar is in your ketchup?" June 2, 2015. https://www.washingtonpost.com/lifestyle/wellness/do-you-know-how-much-sugar-is-in-your-ketchup/2015/06/02/9496b77e-fe5f-11e4-833c-a2de05b6b2a4_story.html

New York Times. "The Case for a Breakfast Feast." August 21, 2017. https://www.nytimes.com/2017/08/21/well/eat/the-case-for-a-breakfast-feast.html

National Health Service UK. "Early lunchers lose more weight, study finds." January 30, 2013. https://www.nhs.uk/news/food-and-diet/early-lunchers-lose-more-weight-study-finds/

NPR. "Eat For 10 Hours. Fast For 14. This Daily Habit Prompts Weight Loss, Study Finds." December 8, 2019. https://www.npr.org/sections/thesalt/2019/12/08/785142534/eat-for-10-hours-fast-for-14-this-daily-habit-prompts-weight-loss-study-finds?t=1584809674976

Nagumo, Yoshinori, MD. Being Hungry Makes You Healthy. Sunmark Publishing, 2012.

University of Michigan: Michigan Health. "Intermittent Fasting: Is it Right for You?" July 29, 2019. https://healthblog.uofmhealth.org/wellness-prevention/intermittent-fasting-it-right-for-you

Zoomer. "'Lifespan' Author David A. Sinclair on Exercise, Fasting and Reverse Aging." October 2, 2019. https://www.everythingzoomer.com/health/2019/10/02/lifespan-author-david-a-sinclair-on-exercise-reverse-aging-and-fasting/

Atlanta Journal-Constitution. "Start intermittent fasting if you want to live longer, study says." September 7, 2018. https://www.ajc.com/news/world/start-intermittent-fasting-you-want-live-longer-study-says/GASdXbaydGMGKLnSIhpoRI/

Harper's Bazaar. "9 Celebrities Who Swear By Intermittent Fasting." December 19, 2019. https://www.harpersbazaar.com.au/health-fitness/intermittent-fasting-celebrities-19484

New York Times. "Sugary Drinks Tied to Shorter Life Span." March 21, 2019. https://www.nytimes.com/2019/03/21/well/eat/sugary-drinks-tied-to-shorter-life-span.html

The Week. "Alcohol and coffee make you live longer, finds almost-too-good-to-be-true study." February 23, 2018. https://theweek.com/speedreads/757101/alcohol-coffee-make-live-longer-finds-almosttoogoodtobetrue-study

CHAPTER 4: FOODS TO EAT FOR LONGEVITY

The Journal of Nutrition. "Carotenoid absorption from salad and salsa by humans is enhanced by the addition of avocado or avocado oil." March, 2005. https://www.ncbi.nlm.nih.gov/pubmed/15735074

Physicians Committee for Responsible Medicine. "High-Fiber Diets Increase Lifespan." January 14, 2015. https://www.pcrm.org/news/health-nutrition/high-fiber-diets-increase-lifespan

The Journal of Nutrition. "Defatted avocado pulp reduces body weight and total hepatic fat but increases plasma cholesterol in male rats fed diets with cholesterol." July, 2002. https://www.ncbi.nlm.nih.gov/pubmed/12097685

MyFitnessPal. "Why Eating Avocados May Help You Live Longer." December 21, 2019. https://blog.myfitnesspal.com/avocados-metabolism/

Wiley Online Library: Phytotherapy Research. "Effects of Avocado (Persea americana) on Metabolic Syndrome: A Comprehensive Systematic Review." June, 2017. https://onlinelibrary.wiley.com/doi/full/10.1002/ptr.5805

WebMD. "Fish, Flaxseed May Lower Alzheimer's Risk." May 2, 2012. https://www.webmd.com/alzheimers/news/20120502/fish-flaxseed-may-lower-alzheimers-risk#1

Healthline. "6 Benefits of Flaxseed Oil – Plus How to Use It." September 29, 2017. https://www.healthline.com/nutrition/flaxseed-oil-benefits

Health Alkaline. "Miranda Kerr Diet – Alkaline Foods – Victoria's Secret Model Diet." March 9, 2011. https://www.healthalkaline.com/victorias-secret-model-miranda-kerr-alkaline-food-diet/

WebMD. "The Amazingly Delicious (and Healthy) Artichoke." February 15, 2010. https://www.webmd.com/diet/features/amazingly-delicious-healthy-artichoke

ScienceDaily. "Largest USDA Study Of Food Antioxidants Reveals Best Sources." June 17, 2004. https://www.sciencedaily.com/releases/2004/06/040617080908.htm

EBioMedicine: The Lancet. "Inflammation, But Not Telomere Length, Predicts Successful Ageing at Extreme Old Age: A Longitudinal Study of Semi-supercentenarians." July 30, 2015. https://www.thelancet.com/journals/ebiom/article/PIIS2352-3964(15)30081-5/fulltext

Journal of Agricultural and Food Chemistry. "Flavonoid Content of U.S. Fruits, Vegetables, and Nuts." 2006. https://www.ars.usda.gov/ARSUserFiles/80400525/Articles/JAFC54_9966-9977Flavonoid.pdf

Harvard Health Publishing. "Eat blueberries and strawberries three times per week." July, 2013. https://www.health.harvard.edu/heart-health/eat-blueberries-and-strawberries-three-times-per-week

Medical News Today. "How can antioxidants benefit our health?" May 29, 2018. https://www.medicalnewstoday.com/articles/301506

Journal of Agricultural and Food Chemistry. "Procyanidin, anthocyanin, and chlorogenic acid contents of highbush and lowbush blueberries." 2012. https://www.ncbi.nlm.nih.gov/pubmed/22175691

Express. "How to live longer: The one vegetable that could help increase your life expectancy." March 21, 2019. https://www.express.co.uk/life-style/health/1103649/how-to-live-longer-diet-foods-eat-broccoli-leafy-green-vegetables

Live Science. "Broccoli: Health Benefits, Risks & Nutrition Facts." June 15, 2017. https://www.livescience.com/45408-broccoli-nutrition.html

Healthline. "Sulforaphane: Benefits, Side Effects, and Food Sources." February 26, 2019. https://www.healthline.com/nutrition/sulforaphane

PMC: Proceedings of the Royal Society B: Biological Sciences. "Carotenoids, oxidative stress and female mating preference for longer lived males." July, 2007 https://www.ncbi.nlm.nih.gov/pmc/articles/PMC2169282/

Oxford Academic: The American Journal of Clinical Nutrition. "Fruit and vegetable consumption and all-cause mortality: a dose-response analysis." August, 2013. https://academic.oup.com/ajcn/article/98/2/454/4577240

Today's Dietician: RD Lounge. "Living to Age 100: Are Fermented Foods the Answer?" September 29, 2016. https://rdlounge.com/2016/09/29/living-to-age-100-are-fermented-foods-the-answer/

Health. "World's Healthiest Foods: Kimchi (Korea)." March 11, 2016. https://www.health.com/health/article/0%2C%2C20410300%2C00.html

Harvard Health Publishing. "Fermented foods can add depth to your diet." July, 2018. https://www.health.harvard.edu/staying-healthy/fermented-foods-can-add-depth-to-your-diet

Harper's Bazaar Arabia. "Everything You Need To Know About The World's Next Big Health Craze: Kombucha." September 11, 2019. https://www.harpersbazaararabia.com/health-fitness/saba-kombucha-brings-the-next-big-health-craze-to-the-uae

Asia Pacific Journal of Clinical Nutrition. "Legumes: the most important dietary predictor of survival in older people of different ethnicities." 2004. https://www.ncbi.nlm.nih.gov/pubmed/15228991

Women's Health. "Are Lentils Actually Good For You?" April 7, 2019. https://www.womenshealthmag.com/food/a26945633/are-lentils-good-for-you/

EatThis.com. "23 Healthy Foods Celebrities Can't Get Enough Of." February 1, 2016. https://www.eatthis.com/what-celebrities-eat/

Everyday Health. "Is Diabetes Different From Insulin Resistance?" February 12, 2008. https://www.everydayhealth.com/diabetes/type2/diagnosing/specialist/getaneh/diabetes-vs-insulin-resistance.aspx

Everyday Health. "4 Nuts That Cut Your Heart Disease Risk." August 19, 2016. https://www.everydayhealth.com/columns/jared-bunch-rhythm-of-life/nuts-that-cut-your-heart-disease-risk/

Harvard Health Publishing. "Eating nuts linked to healthier, longer life." November 20, 2013. https://www.health.harvard.edu/blog/eating-nuts-linked-to-healthier-longer-life-201311206893

WebMD. "The New Low-Cholesterol Diet: Nuts." February 2, 2009. https://www.webmd.com/cholesterol-management/features/nuts-help-lower-bad-cholesterol#1

Shape.com. "17 of Heidi Klum's Favorite Snacks." https://www.shape.com/celebrities/celebrity-photos/17-heidi-klums-favorite-snacks

The Journal of Nutritional Biochemistry. "Analysis of lifespan-promoting effect of garlic extract by an integrated metabolo-proteomics approach." August, 2015. https://www.ncbi.nlm.nih.gov/pubmed/25940980

PMC: Avicenna Journal of Phytomedicine (AJP). "Garlic: a review of potential therapeutic effects." 2014. https://www.ncbi.nlm.nih.gov/pmc/articles/PMC4103721/

EatingWell. "What Cameron Diaz Eats in a Day to Age Gracefully." August 9, 2019. http://www.eatingwell.com/article/292204/what-cameron-diaz-eats-in-a-day-to-age-gracefully/

The American Journal of Clinical Nutrition. "Sodium and potassium intakes among US adults: NHANES 2003-2008." September 2012. https://www.ncbi.nlm.nih.gov/pubmed/22854410

Hypertension. "Association of sodium and potassium intake with left ventricular mass: coronary artery risk development in young adults." July 25, 2011. https://www.ncbi.nlm.nih.gov/pubmed/21788603

Mayo Clinic. "Glycemic index diet: What's behind the claims." https://www.mayoclinic.org/healthy-lifestyle/nutrition-and-healthy-eating/in-depth/glycemic-index-diet/art-20048478

Medical News Today. "What are the health benefits of buckwheat?" April 26, 2019. https://www.medicalnewstoday.com/articles/325042#health-benefits

Tech Times. "Want To Live Longer? Up Your Chances With A Bowl Of Quinoa Per Day." March 25, 2015 https://www.techtimes.com/articles/42112/20150325/want-to-live-longer-up-your-chances-with-a-bowl-of-quinoa-per-day.htm

Age and Ageing. "New Horizons: Dietary protein, ageing and the Okinawan ratio." July, 2016. https://academic.oup.com/ageing/article/45/4/443/1680839

News.com.au. "'Uptight' Posh Spice only eats steamed spinach." March 23, 2016. https://www.news.com.au/entertainment/celebrity-life/uptight-posh-spice-only-eats-steamed-spinach/news-story/696cc41c7966eea5d120e36793379f90

JAMA Internal Medicine. "Association of Animal and Plant Protein Intake With All-Cause and Cause-Specific Mortality in a Japanese Cohort." August 26, 2019. https://jamanetwork.com/journals/jamainternalmedicine/article-abstract/2748453

Alpert, Brooke. The Diet Detox: Why Your Diet Is Making You Fat and What to Do About It: 10 Simple Rules to Help You Stop Dieting, Start Eating, and Lose the Weight for Good. BenBella Books, 2017.

The Daily Meal. "Sweet Potatoes Are the Secret to a Long Life, Says Family of Oldest Person in the US." May 15, 2018. https://www.thedailymeal.com/healthy-eating/sweet-potato-secret-long-life-oldest-person-us/051518

USDA. "What We Eat In America (WWEIA) Database." https://data.nal.usda.gov/dataset/what-we-eat-america-wweia-database

Mayo Clinic. "Mediterranean diet: A heart-healthy eating plan." https://www.mayoclinic.org/healthy-lifestyle/nutrition-and-healthy-eating/in-depth/mediterranean-diet/art-20047801

Life Extension. "Vitamin C Reduces Human Mortality." March, 2019. https://www.lifeextension.com/magazine/2019/3/vitamin-c-reduces-human-mortality

CHAPTER 5: LONGEVITY TOXINS

New York Times. "Sugary Drinks Tied to Shorter Life Span." March 21, 2019. https://www.nytimes.com/2019/03/21/well/eat/sugary-drinks-tied-to-shorter-life-span.html

Live Science. "Sugary Drinks Kill 184,000 People Every Year." June 29, 2015. https://www.livescience.com/51385-sugary-drinks-global-deaths.html

Harvard Health Publishing. "The sweet danger of sugar." May, 2017. https://www.health.harvard.edu/heart-health/the-sweet-danger-of-sugar

Stroke. "Sugar- and artificially-sweetened beverages and the risks of incident stroke and dementia: A prospective cohort study." April 20, 2017. https://www.ncbi.nlm.nih.gov/pmc/articles/PMC5405737/

Harvard T.H. Chan School of Public Health: The Nutrition Source. "How Sweet Is It?" https://cdn1.sph.harvard.edu/wp-content/uploads/sites/30/2012/10/how-sweet-is-it-color.pdf

BuzzFeed. "Let's See If You Can Pick The Starbucks Drink That Contains More Sugar." May 17, 2019. https://www.buzzfeed.com/jasminsuknanan/starbucks-drinks-contain-more-sugar

Mindbodygreen Health. "Why It's So Hard To Quit Soda & Sugary Drinks (And What To Do About It)." https://www.mindbodygreen.com/0-13427/why-its-so-hard-to-quit-soda-sugary-drinks-and-what-to-do-about-it.html

JAMA Internal Medicine. "Association Between Soft Drink Consumption and Mortality in 10 European Countries." September 3, 2019.
https://jamanetwork.com/journals/jamainternalmedicine/article-abstract/2749350

Pittsburgh Post-Gazette. "Sugar is killing us: Study links sweet drinks to disease." March 30, 2019.
https://www.post-gazette.com/opinion/editorials/2019/03/30/Sugar-study-links-sweet-drinks-disease/stories/201903300027

The Guardian. "Bad diets killing more people globally than tobacco, study finds." April 3, 2019.
https://www.theguardian.com/society/2019/apr/03/bad-diets-killing-more-people-globally-than-tobacco-study-finds

The Telegraph. "Unhealthy lifestyle can knock 23 years off lifespan."
July 7, 2015.
https://www.telegraph.co.uk/news/health/news/11723443/Unhealthy-lifestyle-can-knock-23-years-off-lifespan.html

American Journal of Lifestyle Medicine. "The Hidden Dangers of Fast and Processed Food." April 3, 2018.
https://www.ncbi.nlm.nih.gov/pmc/articles/PMC6146358/

Chicago Tribune. "This is your body on fast food—whether it's one burger or fries every day." March 1, 2018.
https://www.chicagotribune.com/lifestyles/health/ct-nutrition-fast-food-20180301-story.html

World Cancer Research Fund. "Limit 'fast foods'".
https://www.wcrf.org/dietandcancer/recommendations/limit-fast-foods-fat-sugar

American Journal of Lifestyle Medicine. "The Hidden Dangers of Fast and Processed Food." April 3, 2018.
https://www.ncbi.nlm.nih.gov/pmc/articles/PMC6146358/

University of Michigan. "Highly processed foods linked to addictive eating." February 18, 2015.
https://news.umich.edu/highly-processed-foods-linked-to-addictive-eating/

Wikipedia: Generally Recognized as Safe

Consumer Reports. "GRAS: The Hidden Substances in Your Food." August 17, 2016. https://www.consumerreports.org/food-safety/gras-hidden-ingredients-in-your-food/

US National Library of Medicine National Institutes of Health. "Trans-fatty acids and colon cancer." Breastcancer.Org. "Trans Fats May Increase Risk"

ScienceDaily. "Insulin Has Previously Unknown Effect That Has Role In Aging And Lifespan." March 20, 2008 https://www.sciencedaily.com/releases/2008/03/080320120729.htm

Harvard Health Publishing. "Is your salad dressing hurting your healthy diet?" May, 2017. https://www.health.harvard.edu/blood-pressure/is-your-salad-dressing-hurting-your-healthy-diet

The Healthy. "16 Condiments That Are Secret Health Bombs (And What to Eat Instead)." October 3, 2019. https://www.thehealthy.com/food/unhealthy-condiments/

Healthline. "Unhealthy condiments to limit." https://www.healthline.com/nutrition/list-of-condiments#section21

Nutrition & Diabetes. "A systematic comparison of sugar content in low-fat vs regular versions of food." January 25, 2016. https://www.ncbi.nlm.nih.gov/pmc/articles/PMC4742721/

CHAPTER 6: SUPPLEMENTS

PNAS. "Prolonging healthy aging: Longevity vitamins and proteins." October 15, 2018. https://www.pnas.org/content/115/43/10836

WebMD. "The Facts on Omega-3 Fatty Acids." https://www.webmd.com/healthy-aging/omega-3-fatty-acids-fact-sheet#1

Time. "Fish: The Fountain of Youth?" April 2, 2013. https://healthland.time.com/2013/04/02/fish-the-fountain-of-youth/

Atherosclerosis. "Age- and dose-dependent effects of an eicosapentaenoic acid-rich oil on cardiovascular risk factors in healthy male subjects." July, 2007
https://www.ncbi.nlm.nih.gov/pubmed/16879829

The Journal of Nutritional Biochemistry. "Dietary fish oil decreases C-reactive protein, interleukin-6, and triacylglycerol to HDL-cholesterol ratio in postmenopausal women on HRT." September, 2003.
https://www.ncbi.nlm.nih.gov/pubmed/14505813

Nature Reviews Neurology. "Fish consumption, long-chain omega-3 fatty acids and risk of cognitive decline or Alzheimer disease: a complex association." March, 2009.
https://www.ncbi.nlm.nih.gov/pubmed/19262590

Nutrition Reviews. "Potential treatment of human nonalcoholic fatty liver disease with long-chain omega-3 polyunsaturated fatty acids." November 1, 2013.
https://www.ncbi.nlm.nih.gov/pubmed/24148001

European Journal of Cancer Prevention. "Dietary fat, fatty acid intakes and colorectal cancer risk in Chinese adults: a case-control study." September, 2013.
https://www.ncbi.nlm.nih.gov/pubmed/23377001

Harvard Health Publishing. "Should you be taking an omega-3 supplement?" April, 2019.
https://www.health.harvard.edu/staying-healthy/should-you-be-taking-an-omega-3-supplement

ScienceNordic. "Vitamin D prolongs life." December, 2011.
https://sciencenordic.com/denmark-feature-prevention/vitamin-d-prolongs-life/1399716

Cell Reports. "Vitamin D Promotes Protein Homeostasis and Longevity via the Stress Response Pathway Genes SKN-1, IRE-1, and XBP-1." October 25, 2016.
https://www.ncbi.nlm.nih.gov/pmc/articles/PMC5689451/

Medical News Today. "What are the best sources of omega-3?"
https://www.medicalnewstoday.com/articles/323144

Harvard Health. "Do vitamin D supplements reduce risk of early death?" December, 2019. https://www.health.harvard.edu/staying-healthy/do-vitamin-d-supplements-reduce-risk-of-early-death

Lipids in Health and Disease. "Polyunsaturated fatty acids in various macroalgal species from north Atlantic and tropical seas." June 22, 2011. https://www.ncbi.nlm.nih.gov/pmc/articles/PMC3131239/

PNAS. "Iodide accumulation provides kelp with an inorganic antioxidant impacting atmospheric chemistry." May 13, 2008. https://www.ncbi.nlm.nih.gov/pmc/articles/PMC2383960/

Tech Times. "Rare seaweed could hold the key to lower blood pressure, longer life." April 12, 2014. https://www.techtimes.com/articles/5435/20140412/rare-seaweed-could-hold-the-key-to-lower-blood-pressure-longer-life.htm

WebMD. "Ginkgo Biloba: The Fountain of Youth?" https://www.webmd.com/healthy-aging/features/ginkgo-biloba-youth#1

Biochemical and Biophysical Research Communications. "Fucoxanthin from edible seaweed, Undaria pinnatifida, shows antiobesity effect through UCP1 expression in white adipose tissues." July 1, 2005. https://www.ncbi.nlm.nih.gov/pubmed/15896707

San Diego Union-Tribune. "Seaweed provides vitamins, minerals and antioxidants." September 25, 2012. https://www.sandiegouniontribune.com/news/health/sdut-seaweed-provides-vitamins-minerals-and-2012sep25-story.html

The Epoch Times. "Gingko Biloba: A 'Living Fossil' With Life-Extending Properties." June 21, 2019. https://www.theepochtimes.com/gingko-biloba-a-living-fossil-with-life-extending-properties_2959849.html

Institute for Traditional Medicine. "Ginkgo." http://www.itmonline.org/arts/ginkgo.htm

Cellular and molecular biology. "Ginkgo biloba extract EGb 761 increases stress resistance and extends life span of Caenorhabditis elegans." October 2002. https://www.ncbi.nlm.nih.gov/pubmed/12396085

CNN.com. "Ginkgo biloba, a potential to treat heart disease." August 6, 1999.
http://edition.cnn.com/HEALTH/alternative/9908/06/gingko.heart/

Phytotherapy Research. "Milk thistle in liver diseases: past, present, future." June 7, 2010.
https://www.ncbi.nlm.nih.gov/pubmed/20564545

CNS & Neurological Disorders - Drug Targets. "Silymarin extends lifespan and reduces proteotoxicity in C. elegans Alzheimer's model." 2015.
https://www.ncbi.nlm.nih.gov/pubmed/25613505

WebMD. "Milk Thistle: Benefits and Side Effects"
https://www.webmd.com/digestive-disorders/milk-thistle-benefits-and-side-effects#1

Healthline. "7 Science-Based Benefits of Milk Thistle."
https://www.healthline.com/nutrition/milk-thistle-benefits#section7

Bulletproof. "Is NAD+ the anti-aging miracle pill? Here's what the science says." May 17, 2018.
https://www.bulletproof.com/supplements/dietary-supplements/nadh/

Futurism. "Boosting NAD+ Levels May Be the Key to Effective Anti-Aging Treatments, Study Finds." October 14, 2019.
https://futurism.com/basis-anti-aging-nad-booster

Science. "NAD+ in aging, metabolism, and neurodegeneration." December 4, 2015.
https://www.ncbi.nlm.nih.gov/pubmed/26785480

Scientific American. "Higher-Fiber Diet Linked to Lower Risk of Death." January 12, 2015.
https://www.scientificamerican.com/article/higher-fiber-diet-linked-to-lower-risk-of-death/

Healthline. "What are greens powders?"
https://www.healthline.com/nutrition/super-greens#greens-powders

U.S. News & World Report. "What Are Greens Powders—and Do You Need Them?" November 17, 2017.
https://health.usnews.com/wellness/food/articles/2017-11-17/what-are-greens-powders-and-do-you-need-them

Springer Link. "Magnesium Role in Health and Longevity." November 14, 2018 https://link.springer.com/chapter/10.1007/978-3-030-03742-0_9

CHAPTER 7: A CASE STUDY

BBC Future. "A high-carb diet may explain why Okinawans live so long." January 18, 2019. https://www.bbc.com/future/article/20190116-a-high-carb-diet-may-explain-why-okinawans-live-so-long

Big Think. "The Japanese practice that will change your eating habits." July 1, 2018. https://bigthink.com/21st-century-spirituality/the-japanese-practice-that-will-change-your-eating-habits

Science. "Biomarkers of Caloric Restriction May Predict Longevity in Humans." August 2, 2002. https://science.sciencemag.org/content/297/5582/811

NHS. "Lifespan linked to sleep." May 5, 2010. https://www.nhs.uk/news/lifestyle-and-exercise/lifespan-linked-to-sleep/

The Guardian. "Brisk daily walks can increase lifespan, research says." August 30, 2015. https://www.theguardian.com/society/2015/aug/30/brisk-daily-walks-reduce-ageing-increase-life-span-research

HuffPost. "Walking as Meditation: Quiet Your Mind as You Improve Your Health". August 23, 2012. https://www.huffpost.com/entry/walking-meditation_b_1790035?guccounter=1

Business Insider. "Travis Kalanick says he walks 40 miles a week inside Uber's San Francisco headquarters." September 8, 2015. https://www.businessinsider.com/uber-ceo-travis-kalanick-walks-40-miles-a-week-in-his-office-2015-9?r=US&IR=T

The Atlantic. "What 10,000 Steps Will Really Get You." May 31, 2019. https://www.theatlantic.com/health/archive/2019/05/10000-steps-rule/590785/

Express. "How to live longer: Having a nap for this amount of time can help achieve longevity." April 24, 2018. https://www.express.co.uk/life-style/health/950639/how-to-live-longer-nap-sleep-time

Psychiatry and Clinical Neurosciences.
"Sleep health and lifestyle of elderly
people in Ogimi,
a village of longevity." 2002.
https://onlinelibrary.wiley.com/doi/
pdf/10.1046/j.1440-1819.2002.01014.x

Sleep.org. "5 Companies That
Encourage Power Napping."
https://www.sleep.org/articles/5-
companies-encourage-power-
napping/

New York Times. "Take Naps at Work.
Apologize to No One." June 23, 2017.
https://www.nytimes.com/2017/06/23/
smarter-living/take-naps-at-work-
apologize-to-no-one.html

Printed in Great Britain
by Amazon